Every woman I know needs more courage—to make the hard choices that lead to the best decisions. In *Brave Enough*, Nicole invites us to a deeper understanding of Jesus-courage that empowers and transforms our lives. You need this book!

CHRISTINE CAINE
Founder of Propel Women and A21 Campaign

Nicole gives us a kick in the pants (gentle, but still a kick!) to step up our courage and live the lives we've been called to live. And then she offers practical steps to take our giftings further and further!

ELISA MORGAN
Speaker and author, *The Beauty of Broken* and *Hello, Beauty Full*; cohost, *Discover the Word*

Nicole's book helps us see that the life God is calling us to goes far beyond what feels safe. She reveals that what God calls us to do requires bravery. The good news, however, is that Jesus requires us only to be *brave enough*: brave enough to take that step of faith into the unknown, the messy, the scary, the downright ugliness of loving hurting people, the place where we risk failure, and the place that requires vulnerability. Nicole then shows how he comes to meet us there and gives us what we need to live out what he has for us.

SARA POMEROY
Founder and CEO, Richmond Justice Initiative

Life—in all its joy, pain, and complexity—is not for the fainthearted. Raw and real, Nicole shares stories, wisdom, and practical tools that empower us to live in freedom and hold tightly to courage for the days ahead.

JO SAXTON
Co-pastor of Mission Point Church, chair of 3DMovements board, speaker, author

In *Brave Enough*, Nicole gives us permission to be courageous. She challenges us to be confident and dares us to step into the purpose, passion, and potential that God designed us to embrace. It all begins with a daily, authentic encounter with Jesus. With real-life wisdom and authenticity, she invites us into a new adventure of being, living, and exploring the grace and growth of life in Christ.

HEATHER ZEMPEL
Discipleship pastor at National Community Church in Washington, DC; speaker and author of *Amazed and Confused* and *Community Is Messy*

Brave Enough is a call to abandon ourselves—our fears, flaws, and failures—for a called-out life, a life that stands the tests of time and pressures of the crowd. As followers of Christ, we are called out to live bold and free. Christ's grace makes us brave enough. Nicole offers this gift to the church with a challenge to live graciously and courageously. I also love the prayer prompts, journaling, and exercises available throughout the book, as I have found these foundational disciplines instrumental for mentoring and discipleship.

NATASHA SISTRUNK ROBINSON
Assistant director, Center for the Development of Evangelical Leadership, Gordon-Conwell Theological Seminary, Charlotte

As a pastor, husband, and father of a grown daughter, I found that *Brave Enough* speaks to the heart of the real stuff. Life's hard experiences require us to be brave, but some of the more ordinary things require us to be brave too. And while this book is beneficial not just for women, it uniquely speaks to them and offers freedom from many of the fears that put chains on life. It gives them permission to not be Christian superwomen or the people that "the voices" say they should be. Instead, *Brave Enough* offers each reader the freedom to be the person God has made her to be. The insights and encouragements in this book are needed, and they offer us help for living in a culture filled with insecurity by comparison.

DAVID DWIGHT
Senior pastor, Hope Church

A lack of courage holds us back from doing those things—uncomfortable, risky, costly things—that God is calling us to. Nicole Unice reminds us that the One who calls is also the Source of the courage we need. A timely, welcome message at a time when we have Kingdom work to do!

CAROLYN CUSTIS JAMES
Author of *The Gospel of Ruth*, *Half the Church*, and *Malestrom*

Brave Enough is an eye-opening, soul-embracing, spirit-filled book with wisdom on living in the freedom God has called us all to. Nicole challenges women to truly engage their hurts and hang-ups with insight into the daily journey that God wants with us. Through her practical engagement, you will be given invaluable tools to truly get your brave on each and every day. She reminds us that as women, at our core, we are all *brave enough*!

EBONY HALLIBURTON
Lead associate director for women, DC Metro Church

Brave Enough is one of those books that stays with you. As I read, I felt as if Nicole was writing directly to me, opening my broken areas and pouring the truth of God's love and power back into those very spaces. Her words are gracious, understanding, challenging, and life-giving, and you will find more freedom and more courage by the time you reach the last page.

LAURA C. ROBB
Writer and creator of LauraCRobb.com

Brave Enough offers wise, practical teaching for anyone who wants to uncover truth from God's Word. Nicole Unice has lived and learned what it means to be brave enough in the midst of a busy life as a counselor, ministry leader, and mom. She is an articulate Bible teacher who has the unique ability to make scriptural principles understandable. Her stories, examples, and advice will inspire you to apply godly insight in your own circumstances. If you are brave enough to open the pages of this book, I believe it will change your life.

MARY ANN RUFF
Women's ministry director at Hope Church, Memphis

Nicole Unice is one of those souls who becomes an instant friend the moment you meet her. Kind, smart, funny . . . all around likable. She has you belly laughing one moment and in deep, soul-searching conversation the next. Nicole's new book, *Brave Enough*, is Nicole doing what she does best—encouraging, challenging, and motivating us to live boldly and freely the life God has for us.

JENNI CATRON
Church leader and author of *Clout*

BRAVE ENOUGH

Getting over our fears, flaws, and failures to live BOLD and FREE

TYNDALE
MOMENTUM™

The nonfiction imprint of
Tyndale House Publishers, Inc.

NICOLE UNICE

Visit Tyndale online at www.tyndale.com.

Visit Tyndale Momentum online at www.tyndalemomentum.com.

Visit the author at nicoleunice.com.

TYNDALE, Tyndale Momentum, and Tyndale's quill logo are registered trademarks of Tyndale House Publishers, Inc. The Tyndale Momentum logo is a trademark of Tyndale House Publishers, Inc. Tyndale Momentum is the nonfiction imprint of Tyndale House Publishers, Inc., Carol Stream, Illinois.

Library of Congress Cataloging-in-Publication Data

Unice, Nicole.
  Brave enough : getting over our fears, flaws, and failures to live bold and free / Nicole Unice.
    pages cm
  Includes bibliographical references.
  ISBN 978-1-4964-0136-6 (sc)
  1. Christian women—Religious life. 2. Courage—Religious aspects—Christianity. I. Title.
  BV4527.U54 2015
  248.4—dc23   2015010059

Printed in the United States of America

24	23	22	21	20	19	18
10	9	8	7	6	5	4

To my baby brother, Steve,

the first to teach me what it means to be brave enough

CONTENTS

Let us then approach God's throne of grace with
confidence, so that we may receive mercy and
find grace to help us in our time of need.

HEBREWS 4:16

INTRODUCTION

I WANT TO LET YOU IN on a not-so-hidden secret: We are all a little scared. We all feel threatened by riptide emotions that seem dangerous and out of our control. We keep a white-knuckled grip on our ideas of what we must be for the world—and what the world must be for us. We're often afraid of being irrelevant, worthless, or forgotten. We worry about what will happen if we speak up, or what will happen if we stay quiet and rest for even a moment. We are like trapped little hamsters . . . scared into stillness but vibrating with anxiety.

Some of those same feelings recently nagged at me and three of my close friends. We had barely spoken in a month, but it wasn't because we were mad. We were just busy. Between the four of us, we had enough carpools, church meetings, and work deadlines to exhaust Martha Stewart. Plus we had to work around our husbands' travel schedules and then nurse not one kid but three with ear infections. And so we did what women do to maintain their friendships—we exchanged quick hugs in the carpool line and a text message or two, pushing off our own needs so we could keep up with the needs of others.

Finally we found one Wednesday morning to squeeze in a

few minutes over a fancy omelet and coffee. We tried to make up for lost time by just getting right to the good stuff, because when these friends ask "How are you?" they mean it.

Lisa went first. It was pleasantries and all the things we Christians think we are supposed to say, about loving our kids and trusting our God. Then Lisa's bright smile faltered and her voice cracked and she held her cup between her hands to shield her face a little. "Actually, it's been really hard," she said. And Lisa, capable Lisa, together Lisa, Christmas-cards-on-time Lisa, broke down just enough to let us in, to tell us that there are layers of worries with her two sets of twins, with her now-staying-at-home mommy life, with the struggles that come with adoption. And it wasn't like a volcano eruption, just a pin-sized leak in her soul, and she confessed about seeing her own limits and the ugliness in it all. And then Lisa let out a sigh, a confused/frustrated/tired sigh, and said, "I know God wants us to trust him with our lives, but it's *hard*. And sometimes I don't know how to *feel*!"

And because Lisa had been courageous enough to let down her guard, the rest of us opened up too. Elizabeth talked of the surprising joy she was discovering as she read through the Bible for the first time and then ranted for a while about her rocky relationship with her in-laws. Ashley waved off our questions about herself—maybe it was too much for that day. But she listened well and offered encouragement to the rest of us as we cheered and lamented over the everyday stuff that makes up our lives. I tried to fill them in on my hardship du jour, which was largely related to my impatience and my stubborn desire for quick fixes. And Elizabeth said she knew it was hard and Ashley texted me later to tell me she loved me.

As I think back to that day, it occurs to me that not one of us at that table thinks of herself as heroic. We are women who are trying every day to make it, to just—live. But what I see in each of my friends is a woman being *brave*. She is confused and sad at times. Sometimes she is even angry and doubtful. But she is not trying to escape from the highs or the lows. She is growing—even when she fights it. She is choosing honesty—even when it stings. She is trying to follow Jesus—even when it's hard.

You might not think your normal life requires much bravery. You might not think *courage* is the answer to right-now problems. But what if courage is the surprising virtue we *all* need? What if your life requires courage?

Some have paraphrased the philosopher Plato, defining courage as the ability to persevere through all emotions.[1] What if learning to hang in there through the fear is the key to the life God planned for us? What if being brave enough to be honest, to name our fears, to face our failures, and to listen to ourselves well—what if those are the first steps toward growth, toward beauty, and toward freedom?

Now imagine this: What if, starting today, *starting right now*, you weren't scared anymore? What if that worried energy were gone? Imagine a life with more joy, more wonder. Imagine if the weight of responsibilities and the burden of failure lifted off your shoulders forever. Imagine what it would feel like not to worry about tomorrow or the next day. Just imagine.

What would you do?

Who would you be?

How would you live bigger?

Would you laugh more, jump off the swings, run that marathon? Would you tell your husband the truth, start that business, join the small group? Would you move on from your past?

What would it take to start living . . . brave?

Brave Enough is an invitation to experience life with courage. This book is about opening our eyes to the ways God is calling us to move beyond our fears into boldness. It's an opportunity to taste the sweetness of grace in new ways, to discover how his love changes how we think, feel, act, and respond in our daily lives. If you've felt that your life is too small, too confining, too complicated, or too broken for an adventure, *Brave Enough* will introduce you to practical, everyday courage that sets you free.

And if you'd prefer to explore this topic in the company of friends, I invite you to check out the *Brave Enough DVD Group Experience*, an eight-session curriculum. The curriculum includes teaching, interviews, and additional questions and exercises for diving deeper into Scripture and walking through the book as a group.

So if bravery conjures up images of Xena the Warrior Princess or Katniss from the Hunger Games, I'd like to introduce you to the *brave-enough* woman. We aren't talking heroics here; we are talking about real life—about the bravery you need to live the life you have *right now*. We are talking about the courage to find honesty, to walk through the tension of a life full of unexpected turns that sometimes bring suffering and sometimes bring deep joy. We are talking about being brave enough to receive grace, to listen and act on God's voice. We are talking about the courage to let go of guilt and to say yes and no with confidence, the courage to live with joy and to leave behind worry. We are talking about being brave *enough*—just brave enough to start living differently. This book is about the courage to be who you are—not who you wish you were.

Let's start there—with the bravery you need to live the life you've been given. And who knows? When you start being just brave enough, you might find your life is far bigger and more exciting than you ever dreamed possible.

CHAPTER 1

Brave Enough

You will never do anything in this world without courage.

ARISTOTLE

IT'S RIDICULOUS, really, I told myself. *Just do it!* I had felt a nudge, a small but holy whisper, to do something I didn't want to do. There had been conflict and I was hurt, and the last thing—the last thing that would even cross my mind as a good idea—was to take another step of reconciliation. I knew that the whisper was from God (because I sure wasn't coming up with it myself) and that what I needed to do was the right thing. And the right thing, on a cold Thursday morning, was to write a note of apology.

I was fighting with God about writing a note.

Because dear friend, let me say it again, in case you missed it: I didn't want to.

I bet you've felt this before too—whether you've said it out loud or under your breath or deep in your heart (as if the God who knows all doesn't hear us when we grumble in our hearts!): There are things that life asks of us, good things, hard things— and sometimes we don't want to do them.

When it came to this note, I really didn't want to write it. I didn't want to with all of my heart. I didn't want to risk being hurt, I didn't want to try to see it differently, and I didn't want to work harder at this relationship. I didn't want to make peace; I wanted to turn around and run. As I thought about holding the pen over the paper, I felt my throat constrict, like my very heart was trying to hold on to those words, not let them become real and flow out of me. I had to sneak them out the side door of my soul, through the pen onto the paper and into the hands of the other. So I began to write; faltering, stopping, and starting again. I thought about what really matters, and I willed my mind to choose the truth and not what I wanted to believe, not what was easier to believe.

I still didn't want to write that note. But something was just a bit stronger than my fear, stronger than my pride, stronger than my own self-created stories. And I believe that something is what we all need—whether we are facing one small act or one monumental leap in our lives.

That something is courage.

The definition of *courage* is "mental or moral strength to venture, persevere, and withstand danger, fear, or difficulty."[1] The root of courage, *cor*, comes from the Latin, meaning "heart." So said another way, courage is a strong heart. Courage is the will to move past fear and get out of our own way, to become the women God has made us to be. Though fear might cause us to cower, courage causes us to grow. Courage is the titanium foundation of our character and the marble-solid pillar of our soul.

Maya Angelou once said, "Courage is the most important of all the virtues, because without courage you can't practice any other virtue consistently. You can practice any virtue erratically, but nothing consistently without courage."[2] Courage is not just a virtue—courage is *the* virtue, the one that stands above all others. Courage cuts across circumstances. We need courage in good times, when God calls us to live in faith. We need courage in hard times, when God calls us to endure.

And although we often assume bravery isn't all that important except in the dramatic, do-or-die moments of our lives, courage is forged in the countless, seemingly-small-but-difficult challenges that everyday life brings us. We need courage to make the everyday choices that become the compilation of who we are, what we value, and how we love.

Sometimes we need courage to write notes, to get out of bed, to say hard things. And yes, sometimes we need courage for the unexpected, defining moments of life.

———

I brought a pint of ice cream and two plastic spoons to the hospital room. Nothing says "Get well soon" better than sneaking in a high-fat dessert. My friend Ellie and I happily passed the pint back and forth as we caught up on life. I had met Ellie when she was in the seventh grade. Even then, she was a compassionate, quiet young woman with a heart for God and for people. Now Ellie was twenty-six years old and twenty-five weeks pregnant, her Young Life T-shirt almost covering her little belly. We were reconnecting—but not over the dilemmas of middle school, like mean notes and hard teachers. Now we talked medical terms—early contractions and steroid shots and stress tests—over the whir of machines. Ellie put on a brave smile, and we prayed together. As I left the hospital room that night, I thought to myself, *She's so young.*

Tucker was born by emergency C-section later that week. He weighed one pound, ten ounces, and had a gap between his esophagus and stomach.

Her little boy is now a toddler, and Ellie now knows what it means to walk through the valley of the shadow of death. She can teach NICU nurses like a pro. She's performed CPR on her son while dialing 911.

Ellie didn't sign up for this life. But she loves her husband and son with the strength of a fighter. She wouldn't have called herself a courageous woman when we shared ice cream, but she's learned to be brave because she had to. God didn't give her any other choice—and now she knows him in a richer, more meaningful way. Turns out, she had just the right DNA for this fight. Ellie's brave . . . *enough.*

—

Sara was working in a call center—a young, single professional planning on a career as a worship leader—when she first heard about human trafficking. She stayed up late one night, scouring the Internet for any information she could get about how organizations were fighting the brutality of human slavery. She was horrified by the videos, so she prayed that night before bed, not expecting God to answer her. But he did. As it turns out, she was part of his plan when it comes to responding to this tragedy.

When I met Sara two years after this defining moment, a lot had changed. One step at a time, Sara had responded to the call. She started a domestic anti-trafficking organization. She eventually quit her job and became a full-time missionary for the organization. She's been awarded grants, has championed legislation, and has begun a prevention curriculum that's being used in high schools around the country. But Sara's job can be lonely and demanding. She's dealt with conflict and confusion and chaos. Yet at every turn, God seems to already be there, fighting her battles and showing her favor.

Sara didn't listen to a podcast on human trafficking with the intent to change the world. But it turns out God had a big plan for a courageous young woman. Sara has learned. She is brave . . . *enough*.

—

When Maria tells me the story about the day her world changed forever, she points out the good things first. She says that it was a beautiful morning and that she and John had coffee and prayed together before he left. She explains that John was running around the college campus where he was a professor—just like he loved to do. She mentions he had no ID with him. She tells how it was unusual that during the day John hadn't called or texted that he would be home late, which alerted her to start looking for him. As a result, many family and friends were at her house when she got the phone call.

She is grateful that she could receive the news of John's sudden and absolutely unexpected death from her father-in-law, who identified John at the hospital and first bore the brunt of the shock. John was forty-six years old and had been a part of her life for more than twenty-five years. They had begun dating when they were both fifteen.

When Maria talks about John, you see the love and the peace. But she twists her wedding rings around her finger when she talks, and I wonder how hard it is at night. Nevertheless, Maria's making it. This isn't anywhere near the life she expected. But she's a courageous woman raising four amazing children. Maria's brave . . . *enough*.

Your Daily Brave

I want to suggest to you that your life—your ordinary life—requires courage too. Whether you are facing a life-altering circumstance like Ellie, Sara, and Maria or an everyday challenge like writing a note of apology, courage is the force that propels us to take a step forward—whether that step is a tiny hop or a desperate leap.

This brave-enough grit is not stereotypical superhero bravery. I'm not talking about the kind of courage that the world loves, courage forged through experiences or knowledge, perhaps resiliency we admire from afar—the kind of resiliency that we hope we'll never need.

This is different, a courage that comes from outside of yourself but that changes you inside your soul. This courage releases the vise grip of fear and gives you the energy and strength and *heart* you need to face whatever life's got for you. Ellie, Sara, and Maria need it because it's these brave-enough steps that have forged their character today. My breakfast buddies, Lisa, Elizabeth, and Ashley, need it because it's the brave-enough grit that's allowed them to be honest. I need it because I've learned that every day presents an opportunity to be brave enough. This kind of courage doesn't come because we are extraordinary in ourselves, but because we have placed our full confidence in an extraordinary God.

No matter what you face today, God offers the same to you. His love—not your own ability or goodness—will be the source of your true bravery and strength. Becoming brave enough to meet the challenges of daily life is where this begins. And when we become brave enough for the small challenges of today, we become brave enough for the big opportunities of tomorrow. Let's explore what this altogether-different courage looks like—what I like to call "Jesus-courage."

> God's love—not our own ability or goodness—is the source of our bravery and our strength.

Jesus-Courage

What exactly do you know about Christ's love? Like me, you can probably sing, "Jesus loves me, this I know." You may even have warm-fuzzy feelings, like Hallmark Channel–movie love, when you hear this song. "Jesus loves me" makes me think of little Dixie cups of apple juice and feltboard Bible stories. But those warm fuzzies can't even get me to be more patient in traffic, much less sustain my heart in the real storms of life.

Of course it is true that Jesus loves us. His relentless passion and ministry spring from love—love for his Father and love for us. But *love*, a word that is so carelessly flung around in our culture, doesn't seem to fully capture what Jesus does for us. Yes, Jesus loves you in your weakness, your failure, and your need, but he also loves you in far greater ways. Jesus loves you into a whole new way of being—a whole new person.

When we examine what happens to people when they encounter Jesus in the Bible, we begin to notice some similarities.

Sometimes Jesus met their physical needs, but he always left them remarkably changed on the inside. They became bold and confident and courageous. I want to suggest that maybe our needs today are not much different from the needs of the men and women who encountered Jesus in person. Neither are the strength and courage that Jesus offers us. Let's look together at the power behind this transforming love.

Take heart

When Jesus came on the scene in the countryside of Judea, it didn't take more than a hot second for people to realize that he was worth listening to. He didn't just speak words—he taught with authority and with power. Word got around, and soon Jesus couldn't go anywhere without hordes of people following him, asking him for miracles, for teaching, for healing.

Once when Jesus was preparing to teach, he went into a house. I would imagine he was speaking in a crowded room where people jostled one another, elbowing and positioning for the best spot to see him. I bet that the room was hot with breath and sweat and that it smelled of people—all hungry to see Jesus, to know him, half-excited and half-frightened about what he might say. And then came a rustling from above and shouts as men pushed their paralyzed friend through the roof so they could drop him right in front of this fascinating man who had been *healing* people—really changing them.

Imagine what it would be like to be that friend. Powerless: unable to move of your own accord. Desperate: completely dependent on others. For years, perhaps even all your life, you've been the outcast, never able to do or be anything—to pull your own weight, to work, to live like those around you.

Perhaps your heart has twisted and guarded itself. Perhaps you pretend you don't care about the stares and the whispers. But it doesn't really matter what you think because your friends insisted that you must see this man. When they couldn't find a way to carry you into the room, they lifted you up to the roof and dropped you down in front of Jesus. Now there you are, in the crowded room, looking up at the faces—faces with expressions that say everything you've ever believed about yourself and about this life, about the haves and the have-nots.

And then it grows strangely quiet. You look up and you see him—*Jesus*. Something in you wells up, something that's foreign and distant. It's been so long since you've felt it that you can't place the feeling immediately. It's . . . *hope*.

Jesus' first words to you are these: "Take heart . . . your sins are forgiven" (Matthew 9:2). Before the healing, before you stand up and walk, before Jesus glorifies the power of God in front of this crowd, he addresses a more pressing need than even *that*. Don't miss this key word in the passage. Our English translation says "take heart," but the original word used here in the Greek is *tharseo*, which simply means "courage." Take a deep breath and take in what Jesus addresses *first*, before he meets any other need:

Courage. Your sins are forgiven.

Be encouraged

Another time, Jesus walked along with a powerful man, a ruler who wanted Jesus to come help him. Even then, people were following Jesus, pressing in on him, shouting his name, needing him. And in that crowd was a woman who suffered from an illness that caused chronic, unmanageable bleeding—a woman who had suffered for years.

Imagine what it would be like to be that woman. Hope was lost so long ago that all you can do now is try to eke out the best existence you can, one day at a time. You are a woman who bleeds, so you are unclean, unacceptable, unwanted. You are shamed for your ailment and discarded for your illness, and you have had to remove yourself from community because you are not allowed around other people.

You are isolated. Alone. Hurting. Desperate.

If you were this woman, I wonder if you could find the strength and the grit and the hope to once again believe life could be different. Would you have the desperate strength to do what she does—to reach out for Jesus' cloak and to touch him and to . . .

Be healed.

The Bible says that "Jesus turned around, and when he saw her he said, 'Daughter, be encouraged! Your faith has made you well.' And the woman was healed at that moment" (Matthew 9:22, NLT).

"Be encouraged" is that same Greek word, *tharseo*. Before Jesus does anything else, he imparts *tharseo*—courage!

Courage. Healing is here.

Don't be afraid

The Bible also tells us about the disciples, Jesus' closest friends and followers. From scriptural accounts, you can almost picture what it would be like to experience the amazing things that they did. Imagine the excitement, confusion, worry, and hope they feel as they witness miracles and listen to teaching they've never known. They are like most of us, a mix of faith and doubt, of power and weakness.

One night, after another long day of ministry and healing, Jesus stayed behind and sent the disciples off in a boat. It was dark and stormy, so the boat swayed and tipped. The wind howled and the waves pummeled these disciples, so even these lifelong fishermen were terrified.

That was some storm.

And in the midst of this powerful disturbance, perhaps the storm of a lifetime, Jesus walked out to them. Walked out on the water, defying the law of gravity and every law of nature, providing his disciples a front-row seat to his power and goodness and God-ness. They were terrified. "Jesus immediately said to them: 'Take courage! It is I. Don't be afraid'" (Matthew 14:27). Here it is again, courage!

Tharseo: Courage.

Jesus is near!

Forgiven sin.

Healed lives.

Powerful presence.

There are only four places in the Gospels where this Greek word *tharseo* is used. Each time, it is spoken by Jesus himself. In John 16:33, Jesus says it for the fourth time; "In this world you will have trouble, but take heart [*tharseo*]! I have overcome the world." Jesus gives us a promise with power. Jesus-courage comes with forgiven sin, with healing, with presence, and with the ability to overcome. Yes, Jesus loves us: he loves us into a completely different experience. He loves us into a new way of living.

What if every single place of frustration, difficulty, worry, or doubt is just a small footpath that leads you to one of these Jesus truths? What if the *obstacle* you are facing today is really an opportunity, leading you right to your own need for forgiveness, healing, and confidence in Christ?

Like the paralyzed man, the bleeding woman, and the disciples, we need this courage. This Jesus-courage is strong, powerful, and steady. It gives energy where we lack it and strength where we are knee-knockingly weak. It is the essence of Jesus himself, the Resurrection power that we have when we receive him into our hearts and allow him to govern our lives.

Jesus gives energy where we lack it and strength where we are knee-knockingly weak.

We can be women who live in this kind of freedom, who confront the dizzying choices and difficult circumstances of life with boldness and confidence. We become these women by taking a journey with Jesus through the darker parts of ourselves, through the refining fire of his healing, and toward the strength and courage we need to follow him. That's an incredible journey, completely worth the shadowy and sometimes scary places we might have to travel through. So we don't go at it alone—we do this with one another and with Jesus, who promises to bring "courage!" for whatever we face.

To help you engage with what you're learning and experiencing, you'll find a variety of exercises at the end of each chapter. These questions are designed to prompt reflection—you might find it helpful to use a journal for your answers.

Together let's get honest about where we really are in life right now—the places where we feel too scared to change, too tired to endure, too weary to persevere, too worried to let go.

Let's take all of that energy and direct it toward God's truth—what he says about who we can be. Let's investigate if this virtue of *courage* can be the catalyst in our souls to compel us and propel us into lives of freedom, love, and, yes—bravery. Jesus did give us a promise: "You will have trouble" but he also gave us his power: "*Tharseo! I have overcome the world.*"

There it is again. *Courage.* It's a Jesus word. And it's everything.

Brave-Enough Pause

Our Daily Brave

Growth starts with honesty. Take an inventory of your life this week. What scares, worries, or concerns you? Do any patterns or themes emerge as you list them (e.g., worries about the future, about money, about what others think of you, etc.)?

When you consider the stories of Jesus-courage, do you relate most to the way Christ forgave sin, healed, or offered his presence? Why is that?

Pray

God, knowing you starts with honesty. I want to tell you how I really am, the places I feel like I'm too worried (or fearful, or needy, or simply too much) and the places where I feel I'm lacking. I don't want to keep acting as if it's on me to make my life work. I want to invite you to be the Lord of my life and have an honest, daily, real relationship with you. Would you show me how to do that every day? I want to trust you.

CHAPTER 2

Brave-Enough Women Get in the Race

*A feeble, nominal Christianity is the great
obstacle to the conversion of the world.*

HENRY VENN

ON A COLD DAY in October, a few friends and I set off on an adventure race called Tough Mudder.

The course certainly wasn't designed for fast times. Picture standing at the top of a very steep off-season ski slope and trying to peer all the way down to the bottom of a brush-covered expanse. Now imagine slip-running down and hike-crawling up that slope several times. Add more than twenty obstacles set along the course, designed to ensure you are bruised, wet, and miserable by the end of each one.

I can't remember which one of us originally thought this challenge would be fun. We had no idea what we were getting into, but we were all competitive enough not to want to be the one to chicken out. Watching YouTube clips of people in earlier races only made it worse, but no one wanted to be the one to claim it was too tough. So off we went.

We scaled twelve-foot walls, dodged fire hoses, and gripped our frozen claws around monkey bars that were set on an incline. By the time we hike-crawled up the first slope, we realized this was not going to be about competition. This was about survival.

About two hours into the adventure, I was freezing and exhausted. We approached yet another water obstacle, one that required ducking under logs while wading through chest-deep water. We dipped under eight logs set across the mud pit, and then we had to shimmy over the final one to get back on land. I put my hands on top of the shoulder-high log and attempted to jump over it, but I barely cleared two inches of water. People all around me were scrambling out, which didn't help my ego, already severely damaged by the entire debacle. I caught a glimpse of my husband, who had been next to me just moments before. He had easily hopped out of the bog and was jogging to catch up with our teammates. In that moment, I felt small and powerless. I wanted to be able to clear that log on my own, but I couldn't. And despite having people all around me, I felt alone.

This is the moment in the story where I want to tell you that my husband's heart leapt in his chest and that our spiritual connection drew him to turn around, race back toward the log obstacle, and rescue me, sacrificing his own time for my gain. This would be the moment when I could draw a Christlike analogy from the adventure race and you could all swoon over my fantastic husband. But I'd be lying, since that's not how this story played out!

Because I am (*ahem*) just slightly independent, I don't really like help. Until I need help. Until I'm standing in muddy water that's probably carrying eighteen fatal diseases and I can't feel my legs and my lungs are constricting and *I'm too short to get over this log and out of the wretched mud pit* and I watch the back of my husband as he jogs away like he's out for a morning run on the beach. And I expect him to know when *I need help* even though I've turned down help for the past two hours and most of our sixteen years together.

As it turns out, someone else helped me out of the pit. Eventually, I did catch up to my teammates, I did forgive my husband (but only after teasing him for at least three miles of the race), and we did manage to finish together. The race was harder than we expected, dirtier than I would have liked, and we didn't finish with an outstanding time—but we did finish. And now it's a story worth telling.

I think an adventure race is a great analogy for our lives, especially when it comes to the invitation to the spiritual life that Jesus offers. The only place to experience life is in the race. Real life happens there, alongside your race companions. You come home muddy and wet and cold and exhausted, but you come home with stories to tell and victories to share. You discover your limitations, you face your pride, and you ask for help. You work together. You find strength that you didn't know you had and encouragement that you didn't know you could give.

But many people prefer to experience life from the side-lines—they talk about the race and about others in the race, but they don't actually get in it themselves. Other people know about the race and even think that *one day* they might run in the race, but they never quite start. Still others sign up for the race but forget that to complete it, this race requires training, grit, and determination.

Failing to get into an adventure race is also a fitting analogy for what happened when Jesus walked the earth. Wherever Jesus was, many spectators followed. He consistently attracted a crowd. Over and over, the Gospels talk about the large crowds that followed Jesus. The book of Matthew mentions over a dozen times in Jesus' public ministry when he was surrounded and pressed on by crowds of people. Everywhere he went, people wanted to be with him. People wanted to listen to him, touch him, and experience miracles. Among the spectators were many who were curious about this "race"—this different life that Jesus proclaimed.

Crowd Mentality

A crowd can be powerful, leading to what psychologists call a herd mentality, when people begin to act alike. It's easy to suspend our own judgment when we are moving along with everyone else. We see it in a dance contest or in a crowd rushing onto the field and tearing down a goalpost. We see it in YouTube videos of flash mobs and rock concerts. Something about the crowd is intoxicating.

Crowd behavior is often funny, sometimes foolish, and occasionally downright evil. The most famous example of herd mentality in modern history was the rise of Nazi Germany, where thousands of Germans were part of the "death squad" responsible for the brutal treatment and murder of millions of Jews. Nazi Germany wasn't a statistical anomaly of evil people in that specific place and time. Rather, we should see this dark spot in history as a warning about how easy it is to go along with the crowd when we aren't brave enough to look at our beliefs and choices honestly—and personally.

Perhaps that's why, early in Jesus' ministry, the Bible says that despite the many who immediately began to follow him, "Jesus didn't trust them, because he knew all about people. No one needed to tell him about human nature, for he knew what was in each person's heart" (John 2:24-25, NLT).

Before wild dancing and goalpost teardowns and Nazi Germany, Jesus was popular. Jesus was a celebrity. It says in Scripture that "great crowds pressed in on him" (Luke 5:1, NLT), that they "eagerly pushed forward to touch him" (Mark 3:10, NLT), that he "couldn't even find time to eat" (Mark 3:20, NLT), and that the crowds numbered in the thousands "milling about and stepping on each other" (Luke 12:1, NLT). I think it's easy to picture Jesus as a serene saint, holding a toddler or petting a lamb, but maybe you should picture someone more like Brad Pitt or Bono. A noisy, loud, demanding crowd of people wanted to be with Jesus *all of the time. He was the popular thing.*

And Jesus was willing to hang with the crowd, the curious spectators who were checking him out. He healed the sick and taught about life. He fed the masses and comforted the people. He suspended his own needs in order to meet theirs. But for Jesus, it was never really about the crowd; it was always about the *he* or the *she.* In crowds, we don't make decisions for ourselves. In crowds, we are more likely to go along than to make a mark. The still, quiet voice of conviction is drowned out in the noise of the masses.

At one point, a large crowd was following Jesus, and he created a distinction between being a curious onlooker and a committed follower.

> He turned around and said to them, "If you want to
> be my follower you must love me more than your own
> father and mother, wife and children, brothers and
> sisters—yes, more than your own life. Otherwise, you
> cannot be my disciple. And you cannot be my disciple
> if you do not carry your own cross and follow me. But
> don't begin until you count the cost."
>
> LUKE 14:25-28, NLT

The offer of life in Christ is inclusive—He invites everyone
to it. Jesus says in Revelation 22:17, "Come!" He invites
everyone who is thirsty to drink from the water of life—his life,
his forgiveness, his healing, his presence. But just because the
invitation is all-inclusive doesn't mean it's easy. Jesus makes it
very clear that he takes our commitment seriously. He tells the
crowds to "count the cost" before they become his followers.

The Greek word used here for *follower* means "learner" or
"student." The question before us is whether we will choose to be
learners and students of Jesus Christ. Jesus
offers us the chance not just to hang with
the crowd, not just to go to church and join
Sunday school or volunteer occasionally at
vacation Bible school, but to be in this wild,
muddy, difficult, incredible race that is life
with him. His invitation is the same now as
it was then: "Follow me."

*Jesus offers us the
chance not just to hang
with the crowd but to
be in this wild, muddy,
difficult, incredible race
that is life with him.*

Are you brave enough to choose Jesus
on the most personal level—in a relationship that's closer than
any other you've ever experienced? How do you feel when you
think about a relationship that's this intimate? Perhaps that

idea sounds a little scary. Maybe you feel vulnerable when you imagine letting someone—anyone—that close to you. Maybe you've been hurt before, or you've never really felt loved and cherished for all that you are. Maybe the idea of a personal, daily, committed relationship that will require all of your heart is a little disturbing. This is why we are talking about courage. Life with Jesus will be incredible—but it won't be comfortable or convenient or easy. This is why we begin by asking whether you are willing to follow him. This is where being brave enough *really* begins.

Many people choose to be distant admirers of Jesus. They are like the crowds who followed him to see what he could do. But over and over again, Jesus offers something different. Saying yes to Jesus is asking him, "Teach me how to do life." Not just life eternal—but life today. Jesus will demand everything from us—and in exchange, we get his life, his courage. This kind of exchange doesn't happen by staying in the crowd. It happens by saying yes to following him—no matter what.

Following Jesus

Following Jesus means more than simply adding another category to your life or another "to do" to your already busy schedule. Being brave enough to follow Jesus every day is like coming to a crossroad and bypassing the easier road of nominal Christianity.

Jesus says, "Whoever of you does not forsake all that he has cannot be My disciple" (Luke 14:33, NKJV). The Bible tells us what it will look like to be brave enough to follow Jesus. These are the nonnegotiables of life with Christ—the truths that are important to know before we begin this journey together. These truths are the way we get off the sidelines and into the race—a journey that's being led by someone else, to somewhere else. It means forsaking yourself as the head honcho of your life and inviting Jesus to be the leader. But what joy awaits those who are willing to follow!

Here are the nonnegotiables of life with Jesus:

Truth 1: Jesus takes you seriously.

I asked some of my Facebook friends to complete the following statement: "I follow Jesus because _____." One of my favorite responses was "because he's the only one who truly gets me."

In his letter to the church of Corinth, Paul explains the depth of Jesus' love for us: "God made him who had no sin to be sin for us" (2 Corinthians 5:21). I don't know how you can get more serious about a person than that. God decided that the very best plan to get back into relationship with us was to send Christ as a sacrifice for our sin since we could not come back to God on our own. I think we could spend our whole lives pondering that truth and still not fully grasp it. God, the Creator of the universe, got together with Jesus, his perfect Son, and the Holy Spirit, the power and presence of God, and they decided they were so serious about us that they would create this rescue plan. This is the good news of Jesus: He does take us so seriously.

Christ made that sacrifice plain to us by going in obedience to the Cross, and he continues to make that sacrifice obvious by pursuing us, over and over again inviting us to leave the crowd and become his students. He takes you seriously. Despite all the ways that you feel you are too much

for anyone—too much worry, too much self, too much failure—you are never too much for him. In all the ways you feel
misunderstood or undervalued, in all the
ways you know that you are hurt and that
you hurt people—you can't shock him
enough to make him leave. We learn that
as we begin to walk with him daily. We
learn it by giving him our whole hearts—
with our whole honest mess—and seeing
him enter in, heal us, change us, and free
us. We learn it through the experience of
following.

Despite all the ways you may feel you are too much for anyone—too much worry, too much self, too much failure—you are never too much for God.

Truth 2: He's serious about what hinders you.

It is almost impossible for us to comprehend the true nature
of God—the fact that he is both grace and truth. Our experiences in life tell us that the full truth about ourselves doesn't
make people love us more; it causes them to reject us. Those
wounds can be like ripples in the waters of our soul, with an
undulating, repeating effect throughout our lives. We hear the
hurtful voices from our early years or our first love, and we act
as if those statements are still true, no matter how old we are.
We grapple with our own regrets and deep disappointments.
When we are in the tumultuous waters of our past, we are not
free! We are just trying to survive.

But here's the thing about God. He doesn't want us just to
survive, to eke out a life as we crawl toward death. He gave us a
life here, and it's not a waiting room. Yes, there is eternity ahead
of us, but we also can experience God *right now.*

So when God reveals himself to us as full truth and full

grace, we have to think hard about that because we don't know anything else like it. We have to watch for it and pay attention to it. We have to experience grace, which we'll talk more about later in the book. We must become attentive to that kind of grace, which often shows up in unexpected places.

My husband, Dave, stumbled across that kind of grace while watching a video clip the other day. He doesn't often get misty-eyed, as opposed to me—who cried the other day while returning a phone call to be someone's job reference. For Dave, tears are rare. In this video, a father accompanies his young disabled daughter as she competes in a beauty pageant. He dances, he prances, he twirls her wheelchair with grace. He then lifts her out of her seat. As he reaches down for her, the girl's usually stoic face lights up with joy, and they finish the talent competition with a waltz around the stage.

As Dave got emotional watching this video, I—being the good former-professional-counselor that I am—snickered a little, mostly because I was surprised at his reaction. When I got myself together and stopped being a cruel and horrible human being, I asked him why he got teary-eyed. He shrugged but then told me it was because of the unhindered, unconcerned show of love from a dad who cared nothing about what he looked like and everything about how his daughter appeared. This show of love brings us to tears, but even that is just a faint image of the grace we find in Jesus. We truly are dis-abled—*unable* to do for ourselves what Jesus does for us. He takes us so seriously that he sacrificed his life so that we might live. If we could fully grasp that love, we would be brought to tears. And if we could stay immersed in that truth for even a moment, we would ask, *What is my response to this great love?*

This powerful love demands a response. Many of us think that this kind of love is a debt we have to repay, and we try to repay it by being good enough. We think, *Okay, this is what Jesus has done for me. Now I will try to prove to him that I'm worth it.* But this is a debt that is impossible to repay, and this is not a transactional love. This love, Jesus-love, is completely different. His sacrifice paves the way for us—not to work harder, but to be free.

Hebrews 12:1 says, "Let us throw off everything that hinders and the sin that so easily entangles. And let us run with perseverance the race marked out for us." Jesus heals us from the disability of our sin so that we can be in relationship with him and run the race he's given us. He doesn't free us so we can strive harder to make life work without him. He frees us to a life with him, a life in which we grow more and more dependent on him even as, paradoxically, we become stronger and braver.

Truth 3: He's serious about obedience.

As we spend more time believing in this kind of love, something happens to us. As we taste freedom—freedom from ourselves, freedom from the ways we feel tied down and tangled up, freedom from our own relentless voice telling us how we must live—we want more. We *want* to be changed. We *want* to pursue the life Jesus offers. We leave behind the idea of repaying a debt, and we actually enter into a love relationship in which we *want* to please the one who loves us. As we take courageous steps behind Jesus, as we follow him every day, we begin to grow. We can't help but be transformed.

God is not on a power trip. He's not trying to get you to do things so that he can prove he's right and you're wrong. He's not trying to get you to obey so he can feel good about himself. He's not a control freak. He is a perfect picture of freedom and protection. He permits you to live the way you want, but when you realize that living out of your sinful nature is enslaving, he rescues you.

This is where we can get confused about what true freedom looks like. Jesus doesn't liberate us to permissiveness; he frees us to a life that makes sense. In his Kingdom there is no condemnation, but there are commands. When we fully grasp how draining life is when we try to live it for ourselves and in our own way, we want to know how God wants us to live. Perhaps this is what Jesus meant when he said, "If you love Me, you will keep My commandments" (John 14:15, NASB). Another way to say that might be "If you've realized that your way isn't working, you'll come do it my way." It would not be loving for Jesus to free us from our own way of living without providing us with a new way of living.

And this is exactly what Jesus does. He doesn't just transact a deal with us—his life for our freedom. He isn't transactional at all; he's relational. So he says to us, "I have set you free, now come be *with* me; come learn *from* me."

Jesus Makes You Brave

This is how much you mean to Jesus. He takes you seriously, he takes the things that hinder you seriously, and he takes your obedience seriously. When he lived on earth, Jesus responded to people individually, even in the midst of the ever-present crowds calling to him, following him, fascinated by him. He responds to us today on a personal level. He is interested in what *you* think of him, not what the crowd thinks.

There are all kinds of reasons that people claim allegiance to Jesus. There are reasons why your friends go to church (or not), why they read the Bible (or not), why they center their lives on Jesus' way (or not). But when it comes to his relationship with you, God is not interested in what your husband or kids think, nor what your neighbors, Bible study leader, pastor, or even that woman who seems to have it all together thinks. He cares about what *you* think. He cares about why you follow him. He wants to walk with you through your unique story—the hurts from your past, the worries in your present, the dreams for your future. He takes you seriously because he loves you, and that love requires a response.

The problem with staying in the crowd is that you don't experience the richest part of relationship and life together. You can't get in the race if you don't take your personal life with Jesus seriously. You aren't really walking with Christ until you are interested in asking the question, "What does following Jesus mean to me?"

You should expect to be changed by Jesus. You should expect to be transformed in the Kingdom of God. The way you think about yourself, the impulses you act upon, the decisions you make—every part of you will be changed by the love of Jesus Christ. Walking with Christ brings you more freedom, more compassion, more courage. Following Jesus fulfills your heart's deepest desires—to be forgiven, healed, chosen, and known. All of your needs are met in Christ, the all-sufficient Savior. This is the promise of life with Christ. It is not an easy road, but it's a rewarding one. And it's the one sure path to becoming brave enough for the race you're meant to run.

Brave-Enough Pause

Our Daily Brave

Whether you've been following Jesus for years or are just getting started, clarifying questions are a helpful diagnostic to become braver. Think about your past week. How was your relationship with Jesus part (or not part) of your everyday life? What are you scared to let Jesus have control of in your life?

Pray

In Luke 9:20, Jesus asked his disciples, "What about you? . . . Who do you say I am?" If Jesus posed that very same question to you, what would you tell him? You can start by saying, *Jesus, I want to be honest with you about who you are to me . . .*

CHAPTER 3

Brave-Enough Women Embrace Spiritual Survival Skills

Disciplines . . . are not the answer; they only lead us to the Answer.

RICHARD FOSTER, *CELEBRATION OF DISCIPLINE*

THERE ARE THOSE who think first and then act, and those who . . . well . . . don't. I tend to be in the second camp. Like other action-oriented people, it's as if I have a big red button in my soul labeled "Go for it" and a trigger finger. That is great when I need to make a quick decision about where to go for dinner, but not so great when I scrape the car in the ATM lane, start moving a dresser down the stairs without help, or think I can cook chicken.

Deciding to take my eleven-year-old son, Charlie, to England for a parent-child camping trip was one of those impulsive decisions. I kid you not—it wasn't until the day before we left that I thought to myself, *Huh. Me and my kid. Traveling alone. To another country. To camp outside. Is this a good idea?*

After barely surviving my driving on the wrong side of the road, Charlie and I arrived at our launch point for the twenty-four-hour "survival challenge," where the trip leaders divided all the participants into smaller groups. It was at this point I realized that I was the only female on the trip and that we were about to confront some of nature's deadliest challenges: mud, bugs, rain—and no bathrooms.

Charlie, on the other hand, was not too concerned with any of those challenges. He had arrived in a boy's paradise. He had a knife. He had a fire starter. He didn't have to wash his hands, brush his teeth, use manners, or ride carpool. He didn't have to write seven paragraphs about his experience in neat lines using descriptor words and a topic sentence.

An hour into our hike, our survival guides stopped. They turned to us and said, "Quick! You have sixty seconds to determine the four essential elements of survival." The groups began to whisper quietly to each other, arguing the finer points of weaponry, water purification, and fire starters. We reported our answers, most of us agreeing that water and fire were at the top of the list. Our guides corrected us with glee: "water, signal, protection, food." Nobody had guessed "signal"—the quick thinking needed to make sure that you could be found for a rescue.

We had gotten hung up in the details of what we needed without thinking bigger. We had chosen different methods without thinking in the broadest sense about survival. Granted, most of us would have died on our own in about two hours had our cheery British guides not been able to teach us the finer points of foraging, insect eating, and fire lighting in the rain—but I digress. The main point of the exercise was to think expansively and make sure we knew what we really needed.

When it comes to spiritual survival, most of us think very little about what our souls need. We know that we require food and rest for our physical health, but what about our spiritual health? Stumbling through life ignorant of spiritual needs doesn't work, just like ignoring our body's needs doesn't work. How quickly our courage vanishes when we lack the necessities in any area of life!

The Bible tells us that we need to be trained and equipped for spiritual life. First Timothy 4:7 says, "Do not waste time arguing over godless ideas and old wives' tales. Instead, train yourself to be godly" (NLT). The apostle Paul knew that we all have a tendency to talk more and do less—and he reminds us that to experience God, we have to spend time and energy in strengthening our connection with him. Romans 12:2 says, "Do not conform to the pattern of this world, but be transformed by the renewing of your mind."

To experience God, we have to spend time and energy in strengthening our connection with him.

Both verses indicate that we need to *stop* doing certain things (arguing over ideas and conforming to the world) and that we need to *start* doing other things (training ourselves for spiritual health by transforming ourselves and renewing our minds). Before we can confront our fears and step boldly into our daily lives, we need to know, embrace, and practice our spiritual survival skills. They are the essential elements, the foundational practices of our faith that make space for God to make us brave.

Spiritual survival skills enable us to withstand the storms

of the human condition, to dream that life will be different, to confront the droning voice of doubt, and to dig in and hold on in seasons of fear. Spiritual survival skills help us when we reach the end of our own capacity; when we don't like the person we are on the inside. A meaningful spiritual life is the antidote to the inevitable creep toward conformity with the world.

The Bible reveals the essential elements needed for our spiritual survival. They are the building blocks of our life with Christ, the daily practices through which God tells us to take heart, to be encouraged, and not to be afraid. They are:

- Word
- Worship
- Prayer
- Partnership

Let's explore the importance of each of these, the essential elements that release our lives from fear and help us make daily brave-enough choices.

Word: The Gift of Truth

I've chosen *Word* as the primary spiritual survival skill because it is the food and water for our souls. Jesus is called the Word. He also calls himself the "bread of life" and the "living water."[1] The Bible says that in Jesus "we live and move and have our being" (Acts 17:28). Bread, water, living, moving, being. That pretty much covers the *entirety* of what we need for survival.

The importance of God's Word is evident from Genesis, the first book in the Bible, where we read of God speaking the world into being. He creates man and woman and passes on this great power of words to them. God has created you and me with an incredible capacity for language—to express our hearts, our hopes, our fears. Words define us. Words give us the ability to make sense of life. And how intriguing that God gave us this capacity and then encourages us toward a love, a need, and a true *passion* for the words he gives us.

In the book of Nehemiah, we find out what happens when God's people lose access to the Word. In the story, the Jews are rebuilding the city of Jerusalem after a devastating, oppressive takeover decades before by the Babylonians. Now the wall is being restored so the city can again become a place of life and refuge for the people. Under Nehemiah's leadership, the Israelites have come together and secured Jerusalem's walls. When the people are finally settled, Ezra the scribe brings out the Book of the Law to be read in the town square. Commentators believe that because the people had been scattered all throughout Babylon, some of them had lost the ability to understand Hebrew and could no longer comprehend God's words for his people. The Word—the life-giving Word—had been lost to them.

For that reason, the Levites, who were the Jewish teachers, "read from the Book of the Law of God, making it clear and giving the meaning so that the people understood what was being read" (Nehemiah 8:8). Imagine standing in that dusty town square as the words of God wash over you for hours. Imagine how quiet it is, as even the little children silently look into the faces of their mothers and watch their fathers stand stoic and still.

I imagine the tears that begin to well up and spill over as story after story of God's relentless love pour forth, as humanity's true condition comes to life in the story of Adam and Eve and Abraham, and in the accounts of injustice, idolatry, and God's incredible rescue of his people from slavery. Imagine trying to make sense of grace, of suffering, of perseverance, of love, without any previous access to Scripture, without any compass of truth to guide you. For the Jews, finally hearing this truth brings on a full-on cry fest. *Now* they understand what is being told to them. *Now* they understand their own condition. "All the people had been weeping as they listened to the words of the Law" (Nehemiah 8:9).

Yet even as the people stand there, feeling like failures, Nehemiah comforts them with these words: "The joy of the LORD is your strength" (Nehemiah 8:10). He tells them to begin celebrating because now they *understand.* He tells them to stop crying and start feasting. You see, God's kindness leads us to repentance and then to rejoicing.

It just doesn't get any better than this! This is the richness of God's Word. I dare you to read it every day. I dare you to read it with these questions in mind: "What does this teach me about God? What does this teach me about people? What does this teach me about *me?*" Author Peter Kreeft says to watch out when you read the Bible, God's living Word, "for when you read it, it is reading you."[2]

Do you know that it takes courage to approach the Bible believing that God has something to say to you? Because sometimes he says hard things. Sometimes his words cut a little too close—like the ones about denying ourselves. Or forgiving our enemies. Or just the simple command "Follow me."[3] It takes courage to read it because sometimes it makes us want to cry—with confusion or conviction or condemnation.

But this ancient story from Nehemiah reminds us that God's Word leads to strength and great joy. We can celebrate that we have this essential spiritual survival element at our disposal. All through *Brave Enough* we are going to talk about Scripture, with plenty of opportunities to engage with your Bible through journaling and prayer. Here's what I would invite you to do for the remainder of this journey. As a brave-enough woman, I invite you to decide, right now, that you want to believe in God's Word for your life. I invite you to take this promise into your heart:

> God has spoken into this world.
> God is still speaking.
> God will speak to me.

What if—maybe just for the time you read this book or are in your book club or Bible study—what if every day you wake up and think, *God will speak to me.* If every time you open your Bible you think, *God has a word for me.* What if you vow to be brave enough to believe it can happen?

Can you imagine how our lives will be different if we live anticipating, supposing, planning—even *expecting* God to speak to us? Can you imagine how bold we will become? The joy of the Lord is our strength—and we are a mighty army when we are joined together in faith!

Just as God's Word brought celebration to the Israelites, it brings nourishment to our souls. Scripture uses the metaphor of food to describe our need for God's Word. He gives us stories—like the one of Jesus feeding the five thousand in John 6—to illustrate that our souls *hunger* for his Word.

He tells us that the physical expression of being hungry and then being filled is akin to our need for his Word—his commandments, his stories, his encouragements in Scripture. He tells the Israelites that he caused them to hunger to create humility—to teach them "man does not live on bread alone but on every word that comes from the mouth of the LORD" (Deuteronomy 8:3).

We have words bombarding us every day that suck the life out of us—so we must make the choice to create channels where we can have those words that put the life into us. Jesus said in John 6:63, "The words I have spoken to you—they are full of the Spirit and life." Jesus' words redefine our problems, revive our weary hearts, and restore our souls.

Deuteronomy 6:6 says, "Write these commandments that I've given you today on your hearts. Get them inside of you" (MSG). The Hebrew word for *heart* is defined as our inner world. One variation on the definition is the "seat of courage." It is from our heart that our actions flow and that we process the world and ourselves and our next moves. We get the Word on our hearts—we place it on our "seat of courage"—so that we can move forward in strength. There is power in his Word, and the more space we make for his Word in our lives, the more we can wield this powerful weapon with skill and strength.

The Bible provides us with "truth, power, life, and joy."[4] *Truth*—about God and about ourselves. *Power*—to step into the fullest expression of ourselves that he's made us to be. *Life*—a living, active agent working to transform us from the inside out. *Joy*—God's words work wonders in even the darkest and most confusing places in our souls. His joy far surpasses our circumstances. It is deep, stable, abiding, and strong. It is our primary spiritual survival resource, and it is the power outside of ourselves that makes us brave.

Worship: The Gift of Surrender

When I was twelve, I had a friend named Wendy. She was a couple of years younger than me, but that didn't matter because she lived in the coolest log cabin. Wendy had a loft in her room and an endless supply of Kit Kat bars. Whenever I would go over to her house, I would first binge on candy bars and then huddle up with her in her loft.

To this day, I have never known another person who was as rabid a celebrity fan as Wendy. She had every issue of *Tiger Beat* and *Bop* magazines. River Phoenix, Corey Haim, Kirk Cameron—their pictures were stuck up on every open inch of Wendy's room. But nobody had Wendy's heart like New Kids on the Block. Her room was like a bad frat party of guys before I knew what a frat party was. She was devoted and dedicated. She was obsessed. She got lost in the music, in the pictures, in her dreams about the next concert and how she *just might* run into Jordan Knight or Joey McIntyre and fall madly in love and become the girl-friend—at least for a video. No matter that Wendy was ten years old—she was living the dream.

God's Word is our primary spiritual survival resource, and it is the power outside of ourselves that makes us brave.

This was my first brush with how we are all made to wor-ship—something that history proves we all yearn to do. In fact, every culture has found something to worship. Today we use the word as slang, throwing it around as a way to express our adoration and devotion to a person or an idea. We even watch a show called *American Idol*. Our hearts are clearly designed for it, and the yearning to worship is one of God's greatest gifts to us.

Worship is powerful because it lifts us out of ourselves. Worship allows our souls to feel weightless, even for a moment. But here's what we know about worship like Wendy's: It never satisfies. Theologian Herman Bavinck once said, "The human heart . . . is so huge that all the world is too small to satisfy it."[5] This world can never live up to the dreams we have for it.

Before we come to Christ, however, worshiping God feels like an absolute offense to our pride and independence. Romans 1 talks about our craving for worship and our propensity to worship the wrong things:

> God shows his anger from heaven against all sinful,
> wicked people who suppress the truth by their
> wickedness. . . . They knew God, but they wouldn't
> worship him as God or even give him thanks. And
> they began to think up foolish ideas of what God was
> like. As a result, their minds became dark and confused.
> Claiming to be wise, they instead became utter fools.
> And instead of worshiping the glorious, ever-living
> God, they worshiped idols made to look like mere
> people and birds and animals and reptiles.
> ROMANS 1:18, 21-23, NLT

While people today may pride themselves in being too sophisticated to bow down before a wooden idol, we still put our hope in some pretty ridiculous things. We give ourselves over to the preteen crush, the fantasy life, the next great relationship or great promotion or great handbag, hoping and expecting that it will meet our needs. We are just like our mothers and grandmothers and our ancient ancestors, distracted and deceived by looking for life in all the wrong places, just like those who "served created things rather than the Creator" in Romans 1:25. Trying to meet this craving in our souls with something tangible and immediate is a powerful temptation, but it has a 100 percent failure rate.

Jesus said that we can approach worshiping God with the wrong motives. We can worship as a twisted way of feeling good about ourselves. We can worship as a twisted way of looking good to other people. But true worshipers, Jesus said, "worship in spirit and in truth" (John 4:24).

Jesus, as always, comes back to the heart.

God desires to have all of you, to draw you into the true worship that your heart was made for. And because God is the only thing in creation that is actually worthy of your worship, he is also the only thing that can truly satisfy your desire for worship.

Worship is a spiritual survival skill because we *are* going to worship something, as surely as we are going to get hungry or thirsty or sleepy. We are wired for it. It's a soul setting that we cannot ignore. And if we don't deliberately set our minds and wills on the worship of God, then we'll just find ourselves giving our devotion away somewhere else.

So what is worship, and how do we hone this skill?

Worship: A definition

Worship is the act of expressing our love. It is our way of saying, "You are higher." Worship is our act of surrender and our reaction to the truth of who God is—his perfect nature, his completeness, his power, his ability, and his mystery. It is our way of saying, "I have only one thing I can offer you, and that is my heart."

Sometimes I feel like worship is the way that I take my heart out of my body and give it to God. I sometimes make this offering sheepishly because my heart doesn't feel like much to give, especially when I sense darkness there. But I know there's nothing else I can give.

Worship is our act of surrender and our reaction to the truth of who God is.

Worship is personal, but it can happen in community settings. Worship is beautiful, but it doesn't have to be done only through song. Worship is as creative as any expression of love can be. Worship can be a letter you write to God in your journal. It can be a picture you draw that expresses who you know him to be. It can be a prayer you pray facedown, hiding in your closet. It can be a song you sing at church and then later in the car and later still in your head, as you sing yourself to sleep. Worship is love. It is getting lost in our love for something greater and higher than us, and the benefits for us are incredible. And here's the best part: Worship changes us.

We so often think we need to be changed by focusing on a particular problem or worry. But the crazy nature of God's work is that transformation happens when we take our eyes off the problems and put them on him. Worship allows us to get caught up in something so big it's beyond us. It lifts our burdens. We may feel weightless in God's presence when we are lost in worship. We experience a lifting and shifting within us—as if God removes our burdens and resettles them in a way that we can bear. We are able to persevere, be joyful, and discover patience for even the most trying situation. And all of this comes as a result of the simple act of turning our eyes away from our problems and focusing instead exclusively on God.

Colossians 3:2 says to "set your minds on things above, not on earthly things." To "set" means to devote. We have to actually use our will, our mind, and our courage to devote ourselves to worship. So often we want to wait until the feeling comes along. We want to worship as an outworking of a feeling, rather than setting our minds to worship and then letting the feelings follow. Devotion doesn't wait for emotion.

Psalm 95:6 says, "Come, let us bow down in worship, let us kneel before the LORD our maker." Romans 12:1 says that we offer our bodies as living sacrifices as our "true and proper worship." Both passages invite us to involve our whole selves in the experience of worship. The psalmist invites us to express our worship through our bodies. The apostle Paul explains that everything we offer in our everyday lives can be an expression of our worship. Brother Lawrence, a seventeenth-century monk, practiced this kind of worship and found it most sweet and intimate in the ordinary rhythms of his day: "Lift up your heart to Him during your meals and in company; the least little remembrance will always be most pleasing to Him. One need not cry out very loudly; He is nearer to us than we think."[6]

Our spiritual survival skill of reading and applying the Word nourishes us, and the survival skill of worship settles us. There is nowhere safer in the universe than in the refuge of God's presence, and every time we worship—whether in song, in prayer, in service, in beauty—we are hidden in him and our hearts are fully aligned and satisfied. As with God's Word, worship unleashes the courage that comes from knowing that God is greater than anyone or anything that could come against us.

Prayer: The Gift of Presence

Yesterday I heard a friend say, "There's not one person who thinks he or she reads the Bible and prays enough." In fact, most of us are easily freaked out by prayer. I don't know if it's because we feel performance anxiety when we're asked to pray or a "never again" stress from bad prayer experiences, but I know hardly any woman who would say, "I know how to pray and I love to pray." But prayer is like the fire starter in our survival tool kit. It sparks change. It shelters our lives by drawing us close to our Father.

When we pray, we open ourselves up to God's examination of our heart. As David writes, "Test me, LORD, and try me, examine my heart and my mind" (Psalm 26:2). In exchange, he brings our heart back into alignment with his will: "Teach me your way, LORD, that I may rely on your faithfulness; give me an undivided heart, that I may fear your name" (Psalm 86:11).

Just as fire has a myriad of uses, so does prayer. But at the core, prayer is communion and conversation. It is the way we spend time in God's presence and understand his will. It's where we confess our sins. It's the vehicle we use to thank God and to bring all of our requests to him. When combined with Word and worship, prayer is an inner sacred space where we learn to listen to God.

We may feel that our prayers are awkward or childish, especially if we aren't used to praying. But we can trust that any prayer offered wholeheartedly is heard. So how do we get to a place of wholehearted prayer? First, we accept that we cannot expect God to act on our agenda in prayer unless we first hear about his. That means praying, as David did in Psalm 26, that God would examine our hearts and lead us to truth. We pray that he would give us clarity and free us from deceit.

Prayer is communion and conversation.

Yesterday as I was praying, I found myself thinking about a project at work. I had posted a project plan up in my office, and for some reason (hello, Holy Spirit) the project kept coming to mind. Elijah encountered God as a "still small voice" (1 Kings 19:12, NKJV) or, another way to say it, as "the voice of fragile silence."[7] This was the fragile, silent voice that asked me why I had posted that plan. First I gave the practical answers—it helps me focus, keeps me on track, etc. But the voice of fragile silence can also be somewhat persistent, and I felt a sense that I wasn't telling the whole truth. *All right,* I said to God in my heart, *am I trying to prove something?*

I could have ignored that little voice and yammered away about my requests, but what kind of relationship works that way? We cannot ignore or avoid something the Spirit says by overriding him with our own voice. Well, actually, *we can do that.* The Spirit is gentle with us in that way. But our hearts need to be brought back to that undivided place.

I had to admit to myself that posting a complicated project plan could also reflect a desire to justify myself. I could prove to anyone who walked by that I was working really hard and was really capable. There was a thread of self-righteousness in it that I hated to admit. But here is the promise of God: When we surrender to that "fragile silence," he leads us into truth and invites us to experience an undivided heart.

So once the Holy Spirit had revealed my sin, the responsibility was back on me, as I confessed my sin before him. This was as simple as telling him, "I'm sorry," although I've found that the more specific I am with my confession, the more cathartic it becomes as I free and unburden my heart.

My admission of ulterior motives was confession. It didn't come with an especially long prayer or in a weird tone of voice. I simply prayed, "Okay, God, I admit it. I think I'm trying to justify myself and appear successful to others." I had to accept that painful twinge that comes with confession, like the increase in pain that comes just as we are about to grab on to and dislodge a splinter. Sin is that splinter in our heart, and opening ourselves up to have it removed can hurt. I could bring all of myself to God, but without confession, I wouldn't have allowed him to do the work he knew I needed.

Not only that, but while sometimes confession is enough, at times action is also required. This is not action in the form of penance or punishment, but the necessary steps that the Spirit leads us to complete so that our hearts become undivided. In my case, confession led to me take down the project plan. At other times, confession might lead to making amends with someone or changing a habit. It might mean agreeing to regularly engage in confession with a friend to keep my heart from going back down the road of deceit.

Hard, real honesty acknowledges that our heart is divided. Confession allows all the disparate pieces to be recognized and organized. That can be tough because when we examine certain pieces of our heart, they usually don't look "Christian" enough for us. Usually the "Christian" and the "good-girl" answers aren't the reality of our hearts, and we divide ourselves even more when we pretend they are. The reality is often more raw, more selfish, more angry, more prideful—more . . . well, ugly. This reality requires help and rescue.

A friend of mine said, "I don't want to pretend that I think God is good and my life is awesome all the time." That's an honest confession, and God can work with that. Jesus Christ is our healer. Honest confession allows *him* to do the healing. And undivided hearts are able to be present with God and to *commune* with him. Prayer is most certainly a two-way conversation, and we'd be wise to let God have the first word. And the last word. And as many words as he wants in between.

God welcomes our whole lives into his presence when we've confessed our sin. With our hearts clear before him, we are able to *converse* with him. "Each morning I bring my requests to you and wait expectantly" (Psalm 5:3, NLT). Every day. "Let us continually offer to God a sacrifice of praise" (Hebrews 13:15). Every moment. Prayer allows us to bring every request in every situation before God (see Philippians 4:6).

God doesn't just allow it—he welcomes it. God isn't a harried boss who doesn't have time for you. He isn't a busy Father who can only give you half his attention. He isn't a slacker boyfriend who keeps his eyes on the football game while nodding along as if he's listening. He welcomes your surrendered heart. He wants your requests. Don't come to him halfheartedly, but instead plunge yourself fully into the experience of his grace and his power. Whether you are reading in your bed or on the subway or at the coffee shop, whatever emotion describes your soul, whatever anxieties fill your brain, whatever stress you carry in your body—right in the place you are, God is available to you.

God offers you his provision, his rescue, his presence. There is a door in your soul, and on the other side of it, you can meet with him. The hallway to that door is an open corridor, a place where you confess your sin, strip off your armor of self-justification and excuses, and just bring the bare truth. There you find communion with God, conversation with God, and confidence in God—the fire starter of our spiritual lives. This is the promise of prayer.

Partnership: The Gift of Others

There was a time in my life when I felt that God had gone silent. I was in full-time ministry by then, so it was all the more disconcerting when I felt I kept showing up for God and he kept missing his appointment.

For many long months, I prayed and wrote and taught into the silence. I kept my head up and kept speaking words about God like they were true, but something began to erode in me during this dark time. I continued to muscle through my faith, to try relying on my own convictions and hanging on to the shreds of stories from my own past or others' experiences, but the outlook was bleak. I didn't see much evidence of God around me or around anyone I "ministered" to. It took me some time to put my finger on what I felt—this heaviness around me—but the word that came to mind was *lonely*. Surrounded by people, I felt so alone.

This would have been the perfect time to reach out, to admit to a friend that I needed help. But I didn't. No one knew what I was going through. It might have been easier to accept help if I'd been facing some life-altering crisis, like illness or death. Maybe if job loss or financial ruin had battered down my door, I might have reached out and told my friends that I needed them. Maybe I would have found someone to pray with me, and I would have been honest and cried. But for several months, I resisted. I tried to go it alone because it felt like the worst kind of failure to say, "My faith is weak."

Yet I was ignoring the fact that without encouragement, we are more prone to wander off the path and lose hope. We need to instill Jesus-courage into one another. Our souls thirst for encouragement, for words of truth and life and grace. In fact, Hebrews 3:13 says we must encourage one another daily so that we will avoid being "hardened by sin's deceitfulness." Brave-enough women make a daily, intentional practice out of speaking words of encouragement and life into the relationships around them.

At what felt like the darkest part of that season, I had to admit the truth to myself, to my husband, and to some trusted friends. Doing so didn't make things immediately better. But it was an essential part of my spiritual growth—and it enabled me to receive life-giving encouragement from those who love me. I believe partnership will *always* have to be a part of our lives together. Remember, all the words we receive and speak can fall into those two categories—life sucking or life giving. And the more attuned we are to what category is which, the easier it is for us to seek out the words of life, to listen closely to them and allow them to soak deeply into our souls.

Friends, nothing in God's hands is wasted because he can use everything in your life to bring others to him. We were made for relationships. We were made to receive from them, and we were made to give to them. It is a spiritual survival skill to learn to partner with other believers through this life.

In a survival situation, people have gone without food for *weeks*—but they can't go forever. That's how I feel about partnership. We can survive for a while on our own. We can believe that we have everything we need, that our faith will hold. Perhaps you relate to my story—finding yourself deceived into thinking your own strength and ability to keep the faith will sustain you. But I've learned we can't go on like this forever.

As author Alicia Britt Chole says, "Jesus does not offer faith for independent study."[8] The spiritual survival skill of partnership comes in two forms: the partnership we enjoy with the Holy Spirit and the partnership of fellow believers.

The Holy Spirit

The Greek word for Holy Spirit is *pneuma* (pronounced *newma*), which means "breath." When we receive Jesus as our Savior, we receive the Holy Spirit as well. He is the divine breath that lives with us and in us. We are invited into communion with the greatest relationship of all time—between Father, Son, and Holy Spirit. Because of Jesus' sacrifice for us, when we receive him, we receive his righteousness, or "right standing." That right standing means we are now invited into the presence of God—into his holiness. The Holy Spirit is the manifestation of God that Jesus promised in John 16:7, emphasizing that it is for our good as humans that Jesus left so that we could experience the indwelling breath of God.

And what does the Holy Spirit do? He is the Spirit of truth. He testifies to us about Jesus. He is called the Comforter and the Counselor (John 16:7). People pay a lot of money for good counselors, and yet as believers, we have the greatest counselor in the universe dwelling within us. We know that the Spirit brings power (Romans 15:13), leads us to life and peace (Romans 8:6), helps us in our weakness (Romans 8:26), and searches the deep things of God and makes them known to us (1 Corinthians 2:10). Those are some incredible offers! So why do we struggle to access the Spirit? It is because of our own stubborn will.

Scripture makes it clear that our sinful nature and the Spirit within us are battling it out. Many verses indicate that we have a choice—whether to listen to our sinful nature or listen to the Spirit. We are urged to "keep in step with the Spirit" (Galatians 5:25) and to "not grieve the Holy Spirit" (Ephesians 4:30). This battle happens all day, all the time. We will always be making the choice to live by our own way—our own sinful nature—or to live by the Spirit. Somehow, in the gentleness of God, he allows us to make that choice.

Perhaps this is why commentators have called the Holy Spirit the "shy member of the Trinity" and a "gentleman." It appears that God continues to allow us to make choices—to have the freedom of will to choose him or not, to listen to the Spirit or not. We have access to the universe's greatest power, and he dwells within us. It is for our spiritual survival that we learn to listen quietly and frequently for the gentle invitation to partner with the Holy Spirit.

Relationships

If I could gather all of you dear readers in one place and asked everyone to raise their hand if they would like a Christian friend to be brave enough with, I think all hands would go up. Some of you would raise both hands. Some of you would be standing next to a Christian friend and still raise a hand. What I do *not* need to convince you of is your need for friends.

But here's the deal with women: We can get really weird about our ideas of friendship. We can lay down all kinds of rules and expectations that the other person might know nothing about. We may be 100 percent positive about what Christian community *should* look like, and we can then dissect the hundreds of ways in which we are currently *not* experiencing that. We long for a wise mentor, a perfect best friend, the most incredible small group, the best dinner club. We want that girlfriend who is just the right touch of sweet and sass, who brings truth and love, who makes us laugh, and who remembers our birthday. She is the friend who encourages us, who calls us before we ask, who doesn't get too needy, and who has perfect advice that she offers only when we ask for it.

If I posted a job opening for the perfect friend, I would never qualify. The standards would just be too high. I could never be that friend to anyone else that I want for myself—so I'm not sure why I'm waiting for that friend to show up for me. It is true that we need one another. But what we don't need is to lay on one another more expectations of what perfect friendship should be. It is God who created us for relationships. He knows you. He knows the longings in your heart. He knows your confusion. He knows the ways you wish you could have that friend who just gets it. He knows you want to be in a super-awesome Bible study or a small group that makes you feel like you can be yourself. He knows you want friends who will accept you just as you are and who will call out the best things in you in ways you can't see for yourself. We are all longing for it. We all want it.

But someone has to go first.

You can be that someone. You can reach out. You can care well for someone by asking questions about her life. You can start that small gathering of women, and you can choose to be the most honest one. You can hold back your judgments about who you think would be your perfect friend and instead ask God to bring someone into your life whom you can strengthen.

Someone has to go first.

Our friends might not come in that perfect package we were expecting, but we can open our minds to the friendships—even if they are unexpected or surprising or not what we pictured— that he chooses for our lives.

Our stormy seasons—like the one I talked about when I felt so alone—are the times when our spiritual survival skills are tested. It is for seasons like these that we are told, "Train yourself to be godly" as 1 Timothy 4:7 says (NLT). If one tool isn't working, we go to another. We fill our daily lives with Word and worship, with prayer and partnership. We use those big umbrella words to capture all the little ways we experience God throughout the day. We whisper thank-yous in the morning, and we lay our needs before him at night. We get into Scripture on a daily basis. We partner with the Holy Spirit and with the body—a church—for encouragement, for learning and relearning about the truth, and for the reminder that we are not alone, that God is much bigger than we can fully imagine, and that he loves us more than we can grasp.

Word. Worship. Prayer. Partnership. These are the spiritual survival skills that instill in us the confidence and joy we need to face any challenge that comes our way.

Brave-Enough Pause

Our Daily Brave

When you consider the spiritual survival skills of Word, worship, prayer, and partnership, which one are you most drawn toward? Which one is hardest for you?

What's something that can spur you on this week? Which survival skill would you like to hone?

If the Word: Commit to read something in your Bible every day this week. You could start by reading Psalms 1–7.

If worship: Add a Pandora station of worship music, or sing a worship song on your way to work each day. See what it does for your mood!

If prayer: Consider writing down your prayer requests. If you begin to journal the things you are seeking God in, you'll also be able to go back and record when God answers those prayers. You'll likely to be encouraged at all the expected—and unexpected—ways God responds to you.

If partnership: Are there a few women in your life with whom you can start a deeper conversation? Challenge yourself to ask a "heart question" of someone in your life this week. Could you be brave enough to even start a book club?

Pray

Father, I do want to take my life with you seriously. You promise that when I seek you I will find you, if I seek you with all of my heart (Jeremiah 29:13). Show me ways that I can allow you to have full control of my heart in all things, whether in joyful times or in challenging seasons.

CHAPTER 4

Brave-Enough Women Love Grace

How few there are who have courage enough to own
their faults, or resolution enough to mend them.

BENJAMIN FRANKLIN

WHEN I WAS IN GRADUATE SCHOOL, one of my assignments was to attend an Alcoholics Anonymous meeting. Let me tell you, for a girl who liked to keep up appearances, that took courage. I pulled into the parking lot of the Methodist church where the group was meeting just as the sun was setting. I wanted a T-shirt that said "Not Addicted! Just a Student" or "Counselor-in-Training." My complete discomfort with the situation said more about me than it did about AA.

I slipped into the back pew of the church as the meeting began. A beautiful, well-dressed woman in her fifties came to the microphone and began to share her story. She was honest. She was funny. She didn't take herself too seriously, but she took her need for Jesus and for recovery very seriously.

As I listened to her speak, I was struck by my own fear about merely attending this meeting as a bystander. I hadn't even wanted to enter the church, for fear of what it would look like to "need" an AA meeting. I realized it takes great courage to admit that we need help. I realized that people sitting in an AA meeting might be braver than most of us.

Thankfully, I've grown a little since then, mostly in my own understanding of how messed up I really am. But here's the problem: Most of us don't like grace. I know—you're thinking, *No, no, I love grace! Grace, like before meals! Grace, like the darling girl's name! Of course I love grace!* Here's the truth: We desperately need grace to be brave enough to live up to our potential, but most of us don't like that we *need* grace.

You might think of grace as forgiveness, kindness, or love. You might think of grace as the patience that allows us to accept one another in our imperfections. Maybe you think of a Bible-word definition—that grace is about the sacrifice Jesus made for us on the cross, which allows us access to eternal life. In some ways, grace is all of these things, but grace is also so much more. To be brave enough to accept the full liberating power of grace, we have to understand what grace does, why we need it so desperately, and how it changes us so completely.

Acknowledging that we need grace is admitting that we have weaknesses we can't fix. It's admitting that there are broken parts in us that are beyond our repair. And I don't mean "beyond repair" as in "Jesus, take the wheel this one time, but then I'll be fine after that." I'm talking about beyond our repair every single day. That's right. I believe there are places in you—and in me—that are beyond our repair. We may have desperately tried to put them back together and then resigned ourselves to our imperfections. Many of us have given up on the idea that the way we live requires great courage and that the way we think, feel, and experience the world matters to God. Many of us are settling for good enough when God is looking for brave enough—brave enough to be different women on the inside and out—because of this remarkable grace.

Many of us are settling for good enough when God is looking for brave enough.

When we come face-to-face with these broken parts of our hearts, our first response is often fear. Fear has no power until we give it control, until we decide that what it says is true and we must take action on it. Then fear becomes the captor of our souls. Fear keeps us stuck and small. Fear makes us treat the world with suspicion. Fear makes us doubt God's goodness. Fear is the little whisper that tells each of us, *Look out for yourself.* Fear sidles up next to us and says, *God doesn't listen.* Fear sneaks in and suggests, *You'll never make it.* Fear says, *God is against you.*

And when those voices get loud, we respond. We might go about our day with distracted and worried minds. We might choose to be silent when we want to speak up. We might ignore our heart's longing for adventure and purpose, and choose the comfortable and known path instead. We might try to justify away our weakness. It's as if we try drinking salt water to quench our thirst. It feels good for the brief seconds it goes down, but it leaves us parched, dry, and desperate.

Fear sometimes drives us to take matters into our own hands. It reminds me of a story a friend of mine once told me about her grandfather, who was fascinated with radios. His condo was full of broken radios that he insisted on keeping, thinking that the transistor from one would fix the other; that he could cobble the broken parts together and make an old radio new. But despite his good intentions—he just owned broken radios.

Our hearts can be just like that—a storeroom of broken stuff, full of mismatched bits and broken pieces. But we keep adding to the pile, thinking that more life experiences will help us sort out and fix all the broken pieces. We are desperately holding out for the one piece we need to fix ourselves. The problem is, the right piece isn't in our hearts, and it's not something we can find on our own. The missing piece—grace—comes from outside ourselves.

Brave-enough women acknowledge that they've tried to fix themselves and yet that hasn't led to the change they seek. They understand that they need something outside of themselves to tell them who they really are, to actually set them free. Remember the story of Jesus-courage in chapter 1? When the paralytic's friends dropped him in front of Jesus, the Lord looked at that disabled man and decided it was more important for him to know that his sins were forgiven than it was for him to be able to walk. Before the paralytic was changed physically, he was healed spiritually. And Jesus told him that forgiveness would give him *tharseo,* or courage. New legs were not the key to courage. *Grace* was the key, and grace still is the key.

Jesus considers our receptivity to his love and forgiveness critically important. It's as if embracing our weak, sinful selves is the actual solution to our problems. He meant it when he said that we would find our life—our full, joyful, free life—when we receive him as the only way, when we receive his gift of forgiveness for ourselves. It's this wacky, upside-down epiphany: Honesty about our failure is the key to courage.

I was talking with a friend about the kind of grit required

to face the truth of our own sin. As we shared stories about how we've come face-to-face with our need for grace, we both shrugged our shoulders about the mystery of it all. Sometimes God draws us to our failures and then seems to serve the ball into our court, giving us the opportunity to get brave enough to change. And sometimes when all we feel is broken, small, and powerless, God arrives right on time with the strength we need to believe in his powerful love and kindness. Sometimes we need courage to accept grace. And sometimes we need courage to act on it. Most of the time, I need courage for both.

Honesty about our failure is the key to courage.

Because it does take great courage to admit that we feel broken on the inside and cannot fix ourselves, we are tempted to try to handle our limitations by ourselves. Sometimes we try to make it better by being okay with our brokenness. When someone bemoans something she has said or done, we like to tell her, "You need to give yourself some grace."

I told myself this as I was driving home from work recently. I was playing out a personal horror movie in my mind, as I like to do sometimes. I was creating ominous scenes of the future stemming from my own failing and sin. I was thinking that maybe being in ministry was ruining my kids and they would despise me as adults. I was thinking of how I wasn't a good enough mom, wife, or sister. I was thinking of all the things I should have been doing that I wasn't, and all the things I was doing that I shouldn't have been doing. It was terrifying. It was a worst-case scenario of how my own actions could ruin the lives of everyone around me. Sound dramatic? It was. You can probably hear the scary movie music playing as a backbeat to these thoughts as I drove home. I finally snapped out of it, interrupting my depressing mental movie montage with this thought: *You need to give yourself some grace.*

Then I had a thought, a thought that ended up being very true and very helpful: *I am unable to give myself the kind of grace I need.*

You see, even the phrase "You need to give yourself grace" leaves Jesus out of the equation. When I'm the one doling out grace to myself, I end up rationalizing why I'm not perfect and how terrible life is. I try to placate myself with some nonsense about "being tired" or "not being focused because I am so busy." I start justifying myself with excuses or start to blame others for my problems. Sometimes I even begin to blame God.

Can you see the problem? This cheap version of grace isn't what my soul really needs. It's nothing like the grace Jesus gives. The sticking point is this, my friends: I keep trying, over and over again, to not actually need grace. I keep trying, over and over again, to fix things myself. I keep trying to manufacture my own grace to repair my brokenness. No wonder it feels weak! My own grace for my own needs is completely insufficient and inadequate for the real brokenness of my soul. The thoughts, feelings, and actions that drive my life have a fatal flaw in them, and justifying, rationalizing, or ignoring them doesn't work. The first step toward receiving real grace is admitting I am beyond my own repair.

The first step toward receiving real grace is admitting I am beyond my own repair.

But beyond *my own* repair is different from beyond *God's* repair. You see, this is where grace comes in. The difference between people who live free and those who just survive is their understanding of their daily need for God's grace. Because when you know personally and deeply the truth of God's grace, fears become smaller. They just do. Fear shrinks in the presence of powerful grace.

As grace increases, fear decreases. It doesn't go away, necessarily, but it loses power. As your heart longs for more grace, more forgiveness, more Jesus-courage, it begins to despise captivity. So if grace means we can't do it ourselves, and grace is the antidote to fear, then you need to be sure you recognize true grace. You need to know the difference between the fake grace you try manufacturing for yourself and the true grace God offers. Let's look first at fake grace.

Fake Grace

Not long ago I was leading a meeting, and about halfway through, little alarms in my head were ringing 911. I knew I was having an internal emergency because the words coming out of my mouth didn't sound like the ones in my head. I was trying to cast a vision for a ministry team, but no one seemed to be getting it. After I finished speaking, I sat down and tried to forget about it, but I couldn't let it go. Then the excuses began:

> *I'm really tired, and I'm not a robot. I couldn't be expected
> to deliver that perfectly.*
> *If my coworker hadn't shared what he did, I would have
> explained the vision better.*
> *I can't believe she asked that question. Doesn't she know
> that wasn't the point?*
> *I wish I had a team that would step it up.*

What ends up playing in my head post-failing is fake grace. Fake grace operates on compromise and concession. Fake grace makes excuses. Fake grace finds problems with others and proposes changes others need to make. Fake grace blames. Fake grace leads us to tell ourselves one of two things: (1) *I'm an essentially good person, so anytime I'm not perfect I have to find another answer. The problem can't be me.* Or (2) *I'm essentially a screwup, so anytime I'm not perfect, I beat myself up. The problem is always with me, so troubles are always all my fault.*

Either way, fake grace creates destructive paths of thought. Those lead to "logical" conclusions about ourselves and others that we continue to live by, day after day. Over time, those pathways become well-grooved, and we find ourselves drawing the same conclusions repeatedly. They might sound something like this:

I'm just stressed out. I need a vacation.
He doesn't understand me. Our marriage doesn't work.
My manager doesn't value me. I have to look out for myself.
I'm too needy. My friends are sick of me.

These patterns of thought usually include an *excuse* and a *concession*. The excuse helps us make sense of our behavior. The concession is our solution for that behavior. This is the way we understand the world. This is the way we understand ourselves. But the problem with this approach? It completely leaves out God.

That may sound harsh, but think about it: The way we worry and turn over problems in our mind again and again—often there is no God in any of it. We live out of fear, not freedom. Our faith is so weak and feeble that God feels far away, maybe even irrelevant to our everyday problems. We may see Jesus as being interested only in rule keeping, or perhaps even irrelevant to daily life. When we manufacture weak, fake grace, we end up being weak, fake people.

Throughout the New Testament, the apostle Paul tells new believers not to forget about grace or try to change it. Accepting fake grace, it seems, was a real problem. In a letter to the church in Corinth, he talks about these new believers believing in a "different Jesus than the one we preach" (2 Corinthians 11:4, NLT). A different Jesus. The idea that we can believe in a *different Jesus* tells us that we must guard our heart against anyone but the real Jesus. So in what ways might you be trying to manage life with a "different Jesus"?

The following assessment may help clarify the ways in which your heart is aligning with fake grace:

Fake Grace Quiz

Answer the following questions with a Y *for yes or an* N *for no.*

1. ____ There are some parts of my heart that feel like they can never be fixed.

2. ____ There are things in my life I've just tried to forget.

3. ____ I sometimes blame others when things go wrong for me.

4. ____ When I'm frustrated by a situation or relationship, I usually think of what I must have done wrong to make it go bad.

5. ____ Sometimes I think God must be punishing me because things are going wrong in my life.

6. ____ I find myself thinking, *If I only read my Bible more [or went*

*to church more or prayed more], then God would answer
my prayers.*

7. ___ Most of the time I think I need to try harder at being a good
friend [or wife, worker, mother].

8. ___ I sometimes act like I have it all together even though I feel
like I'm falling apart.

9. ___ Most people don't know how scared I really am.

10. ___ There are times when I wish God didn't make me the way
he did.

Look over your answers for the following patterns:

*If you answered yes to questions 3, 4, 5: These point to patterns
of blaming.*

*If you answered yes to questions 6, 7: These point to ways you
might have rules for grace.*

*If you answered yes to questions 1, 2, 10: These deal with regret
and shame.*

*If you answered yes to questions 8, 9: These expose the ways
we might hide.*

This quiz is a diagnostic, a way to stir your heart to understand the way you deal with regret, past failures, and current hardships. It reveals how you process who you are and who you can be. It's not comprehensive—just instructive. If you feel a little exposed after answering those questions honestly, take heart. Because every human being desperately needs grace, I believe every human is also prone to manufacture his or her own grace. This might come in the form of stuffing pain or ignoring our past or our failures. It might come in the form of chastising or blaming ourselves or other people for mistakes.

Or it might look like the great cover-up: masking our own insecurities and weaknesses as a way of surviving this life. These patterns of living are the fruit of fake grace.

Still, facing the truth about how we really feel can be pretty scary. Sometimes these honest thoughts make us wonder about everything—about our lives, about ourselves, about God. Sometimes honest thoughts just make us feel worse about ourselves, an ugly shame spiral that we want to escape as quickly as we can:

Escape! Shut the book.
Escape! Check Instagram, get distracted by someone
    else's perfect life.
Escape! Distract myself with worries about the kids,
    or my parents, or my friends.
Escape! Justify. Blame. Hide.
Escape! Change the channel in my soul and pretend
    like that didn't really matter to me.

Sometimes our fears grow louder, so we try to escape in more drastic ways, like when one drink turns into two or three. Or when that friendship becomes more flirtatious than it should. Or when we begin to fantasize about living any life other than our own. These are our souls' natural reactions to a life of fake grace, a life of trying harder—and failing—to make it work. These are also our souls' ways of sounding the alarm, of waving the red flags of distress, to let us know that we need saving.

So though you might feel tempted to escape, I want to invite you to face your fears and failures. When you become honest, you begin to see God work. This deep, hard stuff is where the *tharseo*—the Jesus-courage—comes in. Forgiveness and healing become relevant when you confront the powerful emotions and deceptive beliefs that have been wound tightly into your soul and that make you feel as crippled and broken as the paralytic. It's hard to want healing when you don't feel sick. But if confronting these broken areas is making you feel your weakness, that is okay. Stick with it, because you are getting close to your Savior Jesus, who is so serious about unraveling those chains that he died for you.

If you've been feeling scared or stuck, perhaps now is the time to cast off this fake grace, this *different Jesus*. If this quiz categorizes your life, there is good news! True grace, living grace enters right into our blame, rules, regrets, and escape buttons and brings light where we need it most—in our own dark and limited understanding of ourselves.

This is why brave-enough women love grace. Because they've grown tired of dealing with their problems themselves. They've grown weary of wearing masks and expending emotional energy trying to act as if they've got it all figured out. The escape buttons aren't working. Brave-enough women know they can't make it in this world with fake grace as their mode of operation. If this sounds like you, I want to encourage you to stop right now and pray. Let's keep it really simple. All you need to do is say something like this to our heavenly Father:

> *God, I can't keep doing this on my own. Please show me*
> *how to live in true grace.*

That's it. I believe that if you pray this simple confession with your whole heart, God will begin to reveal his abundant, generous, life-giving, daily gift of grace. It's a prayer you can pray every day, or multiple times a day. It reflects the desire to open your eyes each morning and jump into grace. It's your prayer to say as you close your eyes every evening and welcome the healing power of grace even as you sleep.

Once we admit we don't want to live with cheap, fake grace anymore, how do we recognize the real thing? It starts with a person.

Grace in Person

Jesus talked about two topics a lot: his Father and the Kingdom. God had been referred to as a father in the Old Testament, but Jesus took it to a different level. The way he talked about and prayed to God was totally different from how the religious leaders of the day did. Jesus made everything really *personal*. When he talked about his heavenly Father, he called him *Abba*, which basically means "daddy." When he talked about the Kingdom of God, he said the only way to enter it was to be "born again" (John 3:3) and to receive it "like a little child" (Luke 18:17).

Jesus was telling us that comprehensive life change is possible. Think about this for a second. Imagine yourself as a four-year-old who was just adopted from an orphanage into a loving family. What would that mean for your life? You'd be living in the same skin, but everything would change. Your relationships would become personal and close. Your caregivers had run an institution, but now you have a *dad*. You used to live by rules, but now the primary setting of life revolves around relationship.

Jesus was the living example of grace and the one who made it possible for us to be adopted into God's family. He extended love without condition to everyone who would receive it. He did all the work necessary to restore and reconcile our lives to God. Grace requires all of Jesus and none of us. The only part we play in grace is actually believing that we need it and then receiving it for ourselves. Like the woman who was brave enough to believe Jesus could change her and reached out to touch his robe,[1] we too have the opportunity to be brave enough to believe in this unmerited kindness and unconditional love that's offered to each one of us.

Grace requires all of Jesus and none of us.

So true grace is expressed in the person and life of Jesus. It's not just about Jesus dying for us—it's also about how Jesus lived as an example for us, and about the power of God that is stronger than death. Grace is the comprehensive actions of Christ that allow us to be worthy, free, and right in God's eyes. Grace allows us access to the one place in the universe where our hearts are truly at rest and our souls are truly free: in the presence of our Creator God.

It is so easy to turn away from grace, to make it smaller or less exciting or less important than it is. This has been true since the beginning of time—and it continues to be true for us. Grace is not about getting away with sin. It's not just about being forgiven. Grace is about God's passionate love for you. Grace is like a completely new operating system for your heart. Grace allows you to live out of an inner place where love is the foundation, security comes from the mighty strength of God, and your soul is at rest in his comprehensive promises. Grace changes the way you perceive everything. Grace draws you into a living relationship with God that becomes deeper every day as you enjoy being with him and hearing from him.

In Jesus, "we live and move and have our being" (Acts 17:28). This means that knowing Jesus will impact the way you think and feel. It means that the way you think after you mess up will be different. It means that the way you approach each day will be different. The way you approach *yourself* will be different. Here are four facets of true grace that we experience through Jesus:

True grace is generous.

John 1:16 says, "Out of his fullness we have all received grace in place of grace already given." In his lovingkindness, God always begins by identifying Christ followers as his children. He claims us as his chosen, worthy masterpieces. God gives us the right to be his kids, and then he sets us up for eternity with ways of knowing and experiencing him that will make us have true, abundant life. Grace over grace. Grace first and grace last. Grace in place of grace.

Grace has always been God's approach to his children. Grace first appeared when God revealed himself to humanity. In the Old Testament, God did not reveal himself to the Israelites first by setting rules and telling them, "If you do these things, then you'll know me." No, first God said, "I am the LORD your God, who rescued you from the land of Egypt, the place of your slavery" (Exodus 20:2, NLT). God started with his presence and his rescue. Only *then* did he give the Israelites instructions for life. That's grace.

God, knowing his people couldn't keep the rules, had a plan when his people repeatedly turned away and made their own rebellious choices. We see men and women who wanted to make life work without him, who failed in making it work, and who came back to him again and again. And we see God's continued relationship with his people despite how much they messed up. That's grace.

But in the coming of Jesus, the person of grace, our Father God took it even further. In Jesus, all people received the fullness of God's grace. Jesus came to earth and modeled for us what love and obedience to the Father look like. He was obedient to death on the cross so that he could make the way for our forgiveness—our entry into the Kingdom of God. Jesus came and said, "This is how you do it. This is how you live in my Father's Kingdom." Grace over grace. That's generous.

I had a young friend who recently admitted how overwhelming life felt. She wasn't facing any extraordinary hardships—just the stresses we all deal with. But when she shared with her small group the depth of her discouragement, they went to work. In the space of twenty-four hours, one friend took her kids for the day, another dropped off dinner and a note of encouragement, and a third texted her throughout the day with words of strength and support. That's grace over grace. That's the generous love of God expressed through his people, and all it took was my friend being brave enough to be honest.

True grace edifies.

True grace instructs our lives. To "edify" means to build up in knowledge and truth. And the apostle Paul is a prime example of this result of grace. Paul, first known as Saul, first appears on the scene as a passionate opponent of Christianity—violently and vocally opposing the work of Jesus' followers.[2] But when he encounters living grace in the person of Jesus,[3] he is completely changed. He is on fire for Jesus. There's no other way to describe his passion, his emotion, and his energy. In the book of Acts, we can trace Paul's journeys through Asia and Greece, where he planted seeds of Christianity that eventually spread throughout the entire world. Paul's life was devoted to "testifying to the good news of God's grace" (Acts 20:24). *Charis*—the Greek word for grace—literally means "that which causes delight in the recipient."[4]

Paul preached about this grace—God's bountiful, loving desire to bring us into relationship with him—to make us right. But grace goes beyond that; it *does* something to us. Paul said we live "in grace." He saw "evidence of grace" in communities of believers. When we learn about the good news of the loving-kindness of God, this grace has the power to shift our hearts.

The truth of grace, as we begin to grasp it, becomes the key to unlock a courageous life. When Paul meets with some of the believers and leaders from the church of Ephesus for the final time, he commits them to "the word of [God's] grace, which can build you up and give you an inheritance among all those who are sanctified" (Acts 20:32). Grace builds us into something new and gives us hope for the future.

True grace makes us right.

I was talking with a friend recently, and we were reflecting on how hard it is to just be human. No, seriously. We were talking about our own weaknesses and the struggles we have—our unfulfilled longings, the suffering in this world, and our doubts and fears. She told me, "Sometimes I don't want to be me." I replied, "And sometimes I don't want to be me, either." There is something that feels broken about us, something that feels *not right*. I think that the *not right* in all of us is the expression of sin in the world. We live in a place where things are broken, and that includes us.

So when we talk about grace being good news, it's the best news, because grace makes us righteous. To be righteous means to be made unbroken. It means that the essential elements in our soul that don't work can work again. It means that we have a future where there is no sin—only love. In the future all that is broken inside of us will be made right once and for all. That glorious future is our inheritance—our life forever with God.

But grace is more than our life after death—true grace also provides restoration and renewal within our souls on this side of heaven. It means we can stop trying to repair our hearts and instead fling ourselves into the embrace of our heavenly Father, who tells us to approach his throne of grace with confidence (Hebrews 4:16). Remember what Jesus taught: Be born again. Be like a child. Enter the Kingdom.

The Bible says that when we receive grace, we "reign in life" (Romans 5:17). The power of one man, Jesus Christ, is the source of strength to overcome our fears. We are able to "reign" over every circumstance because our victory and power becomes identified with Christ's victory and power. We no longer look to ourselves as the way to fix things—we look to Christ. And thought by thought, one small action at a time, we bring every part of ourselves under his authority.

True grace is powerful.

Although what's "not right" within us will not be completely changed until we get to heaven, the Bible makes clear that our sin need no longer control us. Romans 6:14 says that "sin shall no longer be your master." Romans 8:2 says that we are "set . . .

free from the law of sin." Colossians 2:11 (MSG) speaks of what Christ has done for us, "destroying the power of sin." True grace reveals to us that although we continue to struggle with sin, we've already won. It's like life is a wrestling match with a strong opponent. We battle and grapple with our own weaknesses, and sometimes we might even feel pinned by the force of our own failing. But we won't lose, no matter how bleak we may feel in certain moments.

Grace teaches us that Christ, who is in us, is stronger than our deficiencies, and together with him, we will prevail in the end. Romans 8:31 says, "If God is for us, who can be against us?" We will wrestle, and we will struggle, and sometimes we may even feel beaten by sin—but it no longer controls us. True grace means that pain will come and sorrow may be near, but we can cry *and* stand in victory. True grace enables us to weather the storms of pain we cause ourselves and the pain that comes to us because we can find refuge and strength in God. In him we discover that the most precious part of us—our souls—are always secure.

We've barely scratched the surface of what true grace is in our lives—but together, the generous, edifying, righteous, and powerful grace of God does one big thing in us—it *transforms* us. True grace means we are not who we once were, and we will continue to be different tomorrow.

First Corinthians 15:10 says, "By the grace of God I am what I am, and his grace to me was not without effect." It is because of grace that I am becoming more of who God intended me to be. It is also because of grace that I'm not through becoming me. This is the power of true grace in our lives.

We may turn to fake grace over and over again, and Scripture reminds us that our heart will turn back and follow our own way if we don't work against it. No matter how far we stray or how lost we feel, the gift of true grace is always ours, every single moment, to turn back to again and again. Remember the statement about the serious nature of Jesus' offer? "God made him who had no sin to be sin for us" (2 Corinthians 5:21). This is our reminder from Paul that Jesus takes us very seriously.

But the very next verse leads us to the "what next" in being brave enough: Brave-enough women take *grace* seriously. Paul says, "We urge you not to receive God's grace in vain" (2 Corinthians 6:1). The Greek word here means "empty" or "hollow." Paul is telling us that it's possible to take on just the shell of grace without any of the good stuff on the inside. We can "receive" it but just hold it, never opening up the gift it is to actually use the contents! The gift might as well be empty if we are going to receive it in vain. Jesus has done all the work of grace, but we are responsible for opening up our lives to this transforming power. We are responsible for admitting where we are wrong, broken, or stuck and asking Christ to reign in those areas of our heart. We are responsible for making the space to hear God's voice and then asking him for the courage to act on his direction.

Sisters, we can't hold on to this grace and then waste it! This grace is our most powerful weapon in the brave-enough life. Grace is healing and power and transformation—changing us and changing the world. How sad that we can walk around with it and never exercise its power. It's like holding on to a fire starter and then never starting a fire—just remaining in the cold. What a waste!

I don't know about you, but I don't want to get to the end

of my life and realize I was carrying something powerful that I never used. I don't want to save God's grace for an emergency, because to be honest, the issues I have on the inside already feel like emergencies! I am not who I want to be. I'm not yet the most free, bravest version of myself. And Jesus Christ decided that it was worth being obedient to the point of death on the cross so that we could receive grace, act on grace, and be changed by grace.

This grace has the power to build us up, to transform us, to break us out of the habits and thoughts that hinder us. This grace makes us brave enough to forgive, brave enough to listen to God's call, brave enough to act on it. This grace is what makes us beautiful, and bold, and free. Let's not waste it for one more day.

Fear keeps us stuck; grace whispers freedom.

Fear makes us suspicious; grace makes us generous.

Fear shouts doubt; grace sings peace.

Fear murmurs, *Look out for yourself;* grace whispers,
You are not alone.

Fear shouts, *You'll never make it;* grace replies, *You already have.*

Fear screams, *God is against you;* grace laughs because *love always wins.*

Brave-Enough Pause

Our Daily Brave

Hebrews 12:1 says, "Let us throw off everything that hinders and the sin that so easily entangles." Imagine yourself right now. (Looking at a picture of yourself might help!) Take a moment to ask God to give you the courage to see yourself as he sees you. Now, imagine the hindrances and entanglements in your life. What are they? What wraps around your heart and binds you? What twists around your legs and trips you up? Take ten minutes to make a list.

Once you have your list, look over what you've written. Then tear the paper up into little bits. Hear the sound of the paper ripping; feel the strength of your hands easily tearing it up. Watch the words become letters and the letters become lines and the whole list become confetti. Throw it away. Now you have a living, real reminder of what God has done with the sin and entanglements in your life. You've taken one step toward freedom. Dealing with your sin isn't as easy as ripping up a piece of paper—but ripping up that paper is a way to acknowledge that God can and will set you free.

Pray

Holy Spirit, you know my list because you are in my heart. You know the entanglements that I wasn't even brave enough to write down. Heal me, comfort me, set me on a right path. Jesus Christ, you came and offered your life for mine so that I could be set free. Help me live in that freedom; enable me to embrace and taste that freedom even in this moment.

CHAPTER 5

Brave-Enough Women Give Grace

I don't have time to maintain these regrets,
when I think about the way he loves us.

JOHN MARK MCMILLAN, "HOW HE LOVES"

As YOU BEGIN LIVING OUT of true grace and building your spiritual survival skills, you will discover that God surrounds you with opportunities to be brave enough to live out of the grace he has given you.

And—ready for this? Most of those opportunities start in the hardest places—right where you are living. With the people already in your life . . . yep, *those* people. The ones who annoy you. The "problem" ones. The ones who have hurt you, and especially the ones whom you've tried to love even though you don't want to be in the same room with them. The grace we extend to others, in other words, is about forgiveness—the intentional choices we make to release resentment and bitterness, even (especially!) when we've decided we have every right to feel wronged.

Jesus said, "A person who is forgiven little shows only little love" (Luke 7:47, NLT). Our own experience of God's love for us, even as we struggle with sin and weakness, becomes the catalyst that impacts the way we love others. In all things, Jesus brings us back to our hearts, the place from which our thoughts, feelings, and actions flow. When our hearts change, we change.

We can see the fruit of our heart transformation in our daily battles to forgive others. Just consider your typical day. You may have to be firm with children who don't want to go to school in the morning before engaging in an irritating conversation with your spouse. You may then be late to a meeting because of heavy traffic, after which you have a hurtful, confusing conversation with a friend over lunch, followed by . . . you get the point. God's love is meant to affect our daily lives, and that starts with how we give grace, especially when we are angry.

Facing anger—and the hurts it stems from—takes great courage. Augustine once said, "Hope has two beautiful daughters; their names are Anger and Courage. Anger at the way things are, and Courage to see that they do not have to remain as they are."[1] Anger is a natural and sometimes even appropriate response to hurt. When we become brave enough, we begin to see that acknowledging our anger is a necessary step before we can offer others the same grace God has given us. Not only that, but when we allow God to change us right in the mess of it, he often displays some of the greatest evidence of his grace.

The Problem with Anger

Here's the crazy thing about anger in women: Sometimes we don't even know we are angry! We women are complicated creatures who often have a hard time understanding ourselves, much less understanding how to explain ourselves to others.

Since Dave and I are raising two boys and one girl, we have many opportunities to observe how different boys and girls are—and then try to interpret gender differences to each other. Here's how that might play out when my husband is baffled by our daughter's loud protests over some minor slight:

> *Dave:* Wow, she sure gets emotional. The boys aren't like this. She's really dramatic.
>
> *Me (in a dramatic voice):* No, she's not dramatic; she's female.
>
> *Dave:* Really? This is normal?
>
> *Me (now scorned):* Do you have a problem with it? What—is she too much for you!
>
> *Dave:* Are you crying?

Now, dear reader, you may be thinking that you aren't like this at all. As a woman who hates stereotypes, I can appreciate that. But stay with me for a bit and consider this: Most women I know share a few characteristics.

We want great relationships.
We care deeply.
We don't forget.

It's no wonder that when someone comes against us, we feel something (anger, frustration, hurt, resentment, disappointment) toward that person. In a study on expressions of women's anger, psychologist Dana Jack noted that when women become angry, it's often caused by the actions of someone close to them, while men are more likely to become angry because of something a stranger does.[2] This is a sign of our tendency to look for meaning and self-esteem in these relationships. So science and our own hearts agree: Women highly value relationships, and when we get scorned (or slighted) by those closest to us, we get mad. And when we get angry, well, that's when it gets complicated.

We women tend to look for meaning and self-esteem in our relationships.

That's because anger can feel scary. It's a powerful emotion that can catch us off guard with its intensity. Anger and our response to anger can be destructive, so our natural response can be to avoid it and ignore it. But when we do, we also deny real hurts, real problems, and real frustrations that need to be addressed. Healing, forgiveness, and reconciliation are available to us, but when we don't face what makes us angry in the first place, we forfeit the healing our hearts actually need.

How We Deal with Anger

I once met with a woman named Denise who was seeking help for her adult daughter. This is a standard approach of women, the counsel-by-proxy idea. I try it myself all the time—expending enormous amounts of energy thinking about how I can fix other people. Counsel by proxy never, ever works, for me or for anyone else, but we all keep trying anyway. So we sat down together to talk about how Denise might be able to ~~fix her daughter~~ fix things with her daughter.

It didn't take long for me to recognize that Denise was really angry. She was disappointed in her daughter's life, and she disapproved of her marriage, her parenting, and her career choices.

She was deeply upset that her daughter didn't care about faith and had rejected Christianity.

So I asked Denise if she was hurt and angry at the way her daughter had decided to live.

And Denise said no.

And she believed it.

Of course, Denise wasn't *just* angry. She deeply loved her daughter and wanted her to live a full and free life. Turns out, Denise had deep regret about her relationship with her own mother and was worried that her relationship with her daughter would be just as rocky. She was also fearful and worried that her daughter's life was going to get even harder because of the choices she had made. *And* Denise was disappointed. *And* she disapproved. *And* she was mad. That's complicated. Sometimes it's easier to try to fix someone else than to stare into the dark and sad places in ourselves.

Depending on our wiring, some of us will readily admit when we are angry and are able to articulate where the hurt behind it comes from. Many women, however, are like Denise and don't recognize the anger that is seeping out of them. Dana Jack's study also looks at how women communicate their anger. Some express anger constructively—by dealing with it directly and talking it out. Other women express it destructively—through physical or verbal lashing out. It can be expressed silently and outwardly, whether by speeding away in a car or punching a pillow. It can be expressed inwardly, by stewing. And it can just leak out of us, through passive-aggressive comments, gossip, or grudges.[3]

But even today, many people in our culture do not consider anger an acceptable emotion for women, so like Denise, we usually try to find different words to express it. We talk about being disappointed, hurt, frustrated, or confused. We talk about being tired, stressed, and misunderstood. We find ourselves eating too much or drinking too much or shopping too much, trying to out-busy or out-numb the vague ache in our hearts caused by disappointment and pain. And there's something else: There's a part of us that doesn't want to let anger go. We want to hold on to our own rights. After all, if we can't make a situation better, at least we can choose how we want to feel about it.

So let's at least admit that we all struggle in some ways with anger and with what to do with it. Let's look at where our anger comes from, what Jesus has to say about it, and the offer of transformation we can experience when we get brave enough to face it.

Sources of Our Anger

Most anger in women rotates around three core issues:

- **Powerlessness:** We feel that something or someone has wronged us or violated a trust relationship with us and we can't fix it.
- **Injustice:** We perceive mistreatment toward others or ourselves and have a strong sense that "it's not right."
- **Irresponsibility:** We have a sense that someone is not carrying their load or doing their part.[4]

I would add a fourth source:

- **Expectations:** We have a sense of how something should go or someone should act, leading us to conclude that "it should be this way" or "you should be this way."

Women tend to express their anger directly less often than men but to hold on to it longer. We may bear grudges, gossip, and manipulate. Think of a troubling relationship in your life right now. You may not think you are angry toward this person, but run the relationship through this filter. Do you feel misused? Do you feel mistreated in any way? Are you experiencing the consequences of someone else's irresponsibility? Do you have an expectation—it might even be an expectation of what life should have been like twenty years ago!—that isn't being met?

If so, you may have an anger problem.

Let's go back to my story about Denise. As Denise and I began to explore her possible disappointment and anger toward her daughter, she began to cry tears of pain, hurt, and confusion—but mostly confusion. I suspect she felt ashamed and exposed, which was foreign and uncomfortable territory. She said to me, "I'm not even sure how I feel." So I gave her a let-it-all-out assignment, a simple way to identify what her heart was really feeling.

If you're like Denise—if you feel stuck but aren't sure why, if you know you have closed off and guarded parts of your heart, if you aren't feeling as full and free as you'd like—you may want to try this let-it-all-out assignment too. It is a starting point for honesty and true conversation with God—it's the beginning point toward growth. This diagnostic tool has no right or wrong answers; it will simply help you know what is really going on with *you*, so that you can invite the Holy Spirit into those places with you.

Let It All Out: The Exercise

Most people experience three major emotions: They feel mad, sad, or glad. I think women are prone to another emotion: fear. If we use these four emotional states as a starting point, we can begin to categorize and understand how we are dealing with life's hardships. When you allow your heart to speak honestly to you, you will get at the truth of what you're experiencing. That is what this exercise is designed to help you do.

One caveat: About five to six minutes into this exercise, most of us will start entering the uglier, dirtier rooms in our heart. We may even want to slam those doors shut because we didn't know we felt that much and we feel ashamed.

Your assignment, if you are brave enough to accept it, is not to condemn yourself. Your assignment is not to stop thinking when it gets hard but to allow the deeper stuff in your heart to surface. Your job is not to interpret or fix what you are feeling—your job is just to *express* it, regardless of how irrational or silly it might seem.

1. In your journal or on a piece of paper, write one of the following prompts across the top:
   "I'm sad about . . ."
   "I'm scared about . . ."
   "I'm mad about . . ."
2. Write whatever comes to mind. It doesn't matter if it's an incident from last week or the last decade. If it's in there, let it out.
3. If you get stuck, commit to spend five more minutes reflecting on that statement. Even if you sit in silence, you are honoring your soul by allowing it to feel what's really going on.
4. Now leave your feelings right where they are. Don't condemn yourself, don't try to fix yourself, don't try to feel differently. Honesty—real honesty—is the first

step of growth, and the first step toward grace. Now that you know what's in your heart, you can bring that honesty into God's presence—not fixed or finished. Now you can interact honestly with God through Word, worship, prayer, and partnership. That's where the healing begins.

Depending on your wiring, you'll most likely have a primary feeling, your "go-to" setting. For me, I sometimes start this exercise with the phrase "I'm thinking about . . ." I know myself well enough to know that I like to deceive myself by "thinking a lot" when really what I'm doing is "worrying a lot." Starting with "I'm thinking about" allows me to then move into the more honest places of fear, frustration, or hurt.

God Lets Us Go First

Now that we've moved toward honesty, we are accessing something beautiful—God's grace in our gritty, undone reality. Most of us find these places in our heart unkempt and unpresentable. But here's where the Kingdom of God is altogether different from anything we can experience on earth. It's in these places that we have the opportunity to grasp onto the truth that God's power can change us completely. There is a miracle waiting for you, and it's in this deepest place of anger and hurt. And it begins with this: *God lets us go first.*

He lets us wander. He lets us simmer in our hurt. He lets us justify our own actions and explain our behavior. He lets us try to do it ourselves. But all the time, he's listening. He's waiting. He's ready to rescue us and take us to a new and spacious place in our souls, a place, as songwriter John Mark McMillan says, where we "don't have time to maintain these regrets."[5] But first—first, he lets us tell him what we think.

In the book of Job, we meet a guy who has every reason to complain. If you think your life is unjust, check out what Job is going through. For reasons unknown to Job—*which God never fully reveals*—Job suffers. He loses possessions and people who are precious to him. He loses dignity and respect, and he is misunderstood. He is vilified by those he called friends, who insist that he must have done something to deserve this treatment from God. And he laments. Oh, he laments! In chapter after chapter, he tells God everything he thinks, every way he's been wronged, every hurt he's felt. It takes him a long time to get through all of his complaints, so it's not until chapter 38 that God essentially says, "Are you done?"

Job is not the only place where we see God allowing someone to go first with honesty. Bible commentators say that Psalm 56 was written when David was being chased down by his enemies, the Philistines. David was literally between a rock and a hard place (he was probably in a cave). In the midst of his words of trust and worship, he said, "Record my misery; list my tears on your scroll—are they not in your record?" (verse 8). Another version says it this way: "You have taken account of my wanderings; put my tears in Your bottle. Are they not in Your book?" (NASB).

What this tells you is that God records your let-it-all-out list. He hears you when you cry. He sees every tear, and he captures each of them, recording the substance and weight of each. He is near to you in your tears. He is near to you in your complaints and in your hurts. He gives you the space to be honest and to open up to all of it—all the feelings and all the failures, all the frustrations and all the places you've written others off in your hurt and anger.

As David noted, God records all the ways we've been hurt and then meets us with truth. He enables us to be brave enough to choose honesty before him, knowing it is the first step to truly finding forgiveness. He then imparts power through his Spirit so that we can choose grace.

Do honesty and tears feel hard to you? They do to me. In fact, honesty can be exhausting. Actually feeling the feelings and letting them come? Actually slowing down to hear from the Spirit what I really think about others? Actually being mindful and present instead of choosing to distract myself with a Starbucks run or Facebook or a good vent session with a friend? Yes, that's what we are talking about.

Yes, this is hard. Honesty of this caliber takes enormous courage. Bravely facing the hard places in our heart and desiring to receive and give real grace takes grit. It takes strength. It might be easier to think of the ways we can save the world than ways we can change our daily life. When we face the fact that we are deeply disappointed with the trajectory of our lives, when we feel the magnitude of hurt we've experienced from someone else, when we realize that we may even be mad at God because we don't feel like he's rescuing us from those who seem to be against us—then what are we to do? That, my friends, is the place we must come to before God will ask us, "Are you done?"

Bravely facing the hard places in our heart and desiring to receive and give real grace takes grit.

While he invites us to be honest before him, he doesn't want us to remain stuck in our self-justified feelings of hurt. Holding on isn't without consequence, whether we identify it as anger or not. How do we know we are holding on to our pain, neither receiving nor giving God's grace for the everyday troubles of life? We are wound up. We are tired. We keep returning to the same hurts again and again. We notice a pattern in our relationships—we frequently feel hurt and misunderstood. Then we keep distancing ourselves. If we are honest, though, we realize we are overwhelmed by the power of the anger and the turbulence we feel inside.

Taking that journey—into the truth of ourselves and our own hurts—takes courage. We actually need to be brave if we are going to sort out how we deal with the slights, misunderstandings, and disappointments we feel in our relationships. But here's why it matters so much; here's why it's worth it: If we love Jesus and want to love him more, he's going to want to deal with this stuff. Jesus took our own sin and need for grace seriously, but he never intended for grace to be a gift we keep for ourselves. It's so good and so generous that Jesus made it clear that we would have to share it. And if we carry all of these complicated emotions toward those closest to us, we aren't living in grace. We aren't receiving it for ourselves, and we certainly aren't giving it to others.

All of us are hit with hurts, minor slights, and deep disappointments every day. So the question isn't *if* you need to deal with disappointment and anger. The true question is *how* you deal with that hurt. Once you know the how, it's easier to identify where you might need to change. And once you experience the kind of change and freedom that God can create in you—changing your heart toward others and toward yourself—you won't want to stay stuck in those old patterns for one more second.

Before venturing into this territory, it's appropriate to recognize how dark it can be in these parts of our hearts. Praise God that he proclaims that darkness is as light to him (see Psalm 139:12)! He can handle this treacherous, murky place in our heart like no other person can. He can bring light to the darkest and most confusing nuances of our relationships. And more than that, in his truth he can bring healing and joy. So if you are willing, if you are brave enough, will you pray a simple prayer like this one with me right now?

Heavenly Father, give me eyes to see where I am deceived by my own anger, and give me the courage to surrender to your truth and your healing.

Why We Have to Deal with Anger

Imagine yourself sitting among a large crowd and listening to Jesus. After making some difficult statements about who is truly blessed and what it means to be righteous, he suddenly says something you can easily nod your head to: "You have heard that it was said to the people long ago, 'You shall not murder, and anyone who murders will be subject to judgment'" (Matthew 5:21).

Oh, good, you think, *he's not talking to me; he's talking to murderers.*

Then after pausing for dramatic effect (at least in my imagination), Jesus says tenderly and clearly:

But I tell you that anyone who is angry with a brother or sister will be subject to judgment. Again, anyone who says to a brother or sister, "Raca," is answerable to the court. And anyone who says "You fool!" will be in danger of the fire of hell.

MATTHEW 5:22

Anytime Jesus remarks, "But I tell you," we are in for it. Jesus was telling the people, "Stop looking at the rules to justify yourself! If you understood the real rules, you'd look at your heart!" The word *raca* was a word of contempt. Using that word to describe someone was like spitting on them. It said, "You are worthless to me. I have written you off."

When Jesus linked murder and anger in this way, he exposed the truth about what happens when we don't deal with our anger: It festers and grows. It breeds contempt. It makes us look at a person and say in our heart: "You are worthless to me. You are worthy of my disdain." Here is the hard truth: As women, we may not express our anger with fists. Instead, we take up weapons in our hearts. We rage and wound and write people off. We may continue to allow them to be in relationship with us; we may even continue to smile and relate and pretend that all is well. We may go through the motions of forgiveness, but inside our hearts, we defend that territory by blocking it off and deciding, *Because of what you've done to me, you are no longer worthy of my true love. You are written off. You are dead to me.*

The Sermon on the Mount changes everything, because Jesus essentially said, "Your words are like actions to me. Your thoughts are like words to me." What we think, feel, and act upon inside is as available to God as what we actually say and do. That's why Jesus made no distinction between anger and murder. Perhaps this is why Jesus' teaching astonished so many people. Jesus leveled the playing field between hearts and hands.

He said, "These people you think are bad? The *murderers*? You are no different from them."

I wonder what it would have been like to have the clear, penetrating eyes of Jesus on me when he said those words. I imagine I'd want to reply, "But do you know about my situation? Do you know what my 'brother' did? What about the injustice? What about judging *him* for *his* actions?"

Exposing that truth feels—well, it feels exposing! I feel both justified and ashamed about my desire to prove to God that I'm right and should be allowed to feel the way I do.

Yet eventually unresolved anger will start leaking into everything and onto everyone. Maybe that's why Jesus spoke so strongly against anger—because he knows what it does to us when we hold on.

But God Really Goes First

I know you may have deep hurts. I know that someone who was supposed to love you may have taken advantage of you instead. I know that perhaps you've been scared and mistreated. I know you may be living in a marriage that feels like pushing a boulder uphill every single day. I know that you may be so sick of yourself you will do anything to escape your own failures. I know that you may be scared to death or shamed to death and feel stuck, lonely, and small. I've heard enough stories to know that forgiveness is complicated; forgiveness doesn't always mean reconciliation, and forgiveness doesn't mean staying in a harmful or abusive situation. But I do know that forgiveness is the absolute heart of God because it is his way of setting us free.

So as I prayed about you and everyone reading this book, I told God I didn't know how to give you steps to forgiveness when life is hard like that. And I felt a sense of God's leading: *Don't tell them* how *to forgive. Tell them* why *to forgive.*

When you find yourself facing your utter helplessness to see things differently, to feel differently, to act differently—then you are close, once again, to the reason Jesus came in the first place. He takes you seriously. He knows you get stuck. He is well-acquainted with your deep need for him and your utter powerlessness to change your situation. Jesus came to set us free from the power of sin in our lives, from the first time we ask him to enter in and be our Lord and Savior, and every time thereafter.

Jesus is well-acquainted with your deep need for him and your utter powerlessness to change your situation.

The Gospel of John gives us some rich stories of what happened just before and after Jesus' resurrection—and how he extended grace, even in his darkest hours. Think about what it must have felt like to be one of Jesus' friends during that tumultuous time. At the beginning of the final week before his crucifixion, Jesus entered Jerusalem riding on a donkey, as great crowds of people waved palm fronds and laid down their cloaks to create a royal processional. The Jewish people were oppressed by the Romans and familiar with injustice—they lived it every day. To them, a savior looked like a military leader, one who would take back what was due them and restore them to prosperity. They thought Jesus was coming to be their king, to make things right that were so wrong.

Yet despite a crowd of people who were drawn to Christ, John tells us that others were repelled by him. Jesus, however, refused to be distracted from his mission. He told the people who came to hear him speak that week, "I have come into the world as a light, so that no one who believes in me should stay in darkness" (John 12:46).

Those listening closely may have noticed that he was speaking about his desire to follow the will of his heavenly Father who had sent him and to be a light in the darkness. This was no ordinary king.

We don't know what the disciples made of these events, but things must have seemed to be getting weirder by the time they sat down with Jesus for the traditional Passover meal Thursday evening. Before they began to eat, Jesus got up and then stooped down to wash each disciple's feet. While it was customary for guests to have their feet washed before a meal, this was a job for a servant or a slave, not for a king.

When Jesus got to Peter, Peter wasn't having it. This disciple had no interest in having his leader/mentor/friend do something so degrading and humiliating as wash his dirty feet. He told Jesus, "You shall never wash my feet." And Jesus said, "Unless I wash you, you have no part with me" (John 13:8-9).

This is grace.

Grace is receiving the selfless acts of Jesus like *this*. Jesus wasn't just cleaning his friends' feet. He was giving them an experience—something they could touch and feel and remember—as a symbol of the way he loved them. He did for them what they would not and could not do for themselves—and in that cleansing, Jesus sent a message, one that wouldn't be fully understood until he went to the Cross.

Another disciple had his feet washed too.

Judas.

After Jesus poured water on Judas's feet, he held them and rubbed them clean.

Once he'd washed all their feet, Jesus turned to his disciples and said, "I have set you an example that you should do as I have done for you" (John 13:15). Just after this, Judas left the room to betray Jesus.

Jesus never rejected anyone. His offer of love and relationship is completely different from our own because it is unconditional. Jesus often said hard things and he always taught the truth, but he never rejected anyone. When the disciples gathered around this table, with all the thoughts of Jesus' coming Kingdom, his new rule, and where they might belong in that Kingdom, they may have had little idea what was coming. I doubt they understood that Jesus would soon die an agonizing, bloody, slow death on a symbol of condemnation and curse: the cross. They had no idea what it would cost for Jesus to offer them the kind of grace that wouldn't just cleanse them for a few hours, but would make them right for eternity.

If that offends your sensibilities, it should. Thinking about those last days in Jesus' earthly life is hard and uncomfortable. It's hard to accept that it took this kind of love to make us right; that it's this kind of love that Jesus tells us is an example for how we should live. It was hard for Peter to accept when Jesus stooped low to wash his feet. It's personal and intimate, and it requires us to let Jesus invade our personal space, our rights, and our understanding of how the world should work.

But this is where it gets good, because though the world fell silent for what must have been the darkest three days in the history of the world, Jesus was not beaten. Though the biggest injustice the world would ever know had been committed, justice still reigned. When Jesus was raised to life, our understanding of justice was undone. All we know about the way the world works, about what real power is, about what it means to live free in this world was completely turned upside down.

After Jesus was resurrected, he appeared to the disciples as they hid out in a locked room. When the disciples saw him, John 20:20 says they were "overjoyed" (which feels like an understatement to me). When Jesus showed them his scarred hands and feet, he joined the injustice of his sacrifice with the joy of his resurrection. He made it real. He made sure they understood that he really had suffered and died, but that the power of God goes beyond the twisted and crooked hearts of men. Even death cannot hold it down.

So what did Jesus do next? He stood right in the middle of them and said, "Peace be with you!" And then he breathed on them. Yep, he had them come close and he breathed on them, saying, "Receive the Holy Spirit." He gave them a tangible expression of new life. That's a God move, reminiscent of Genesis 2:7, which says that God formed man and "breathed into his nostrils the breath of life."

Then Jesus gave them a mission: "If you forgive anyone's sins, their sins are forgiven; if you do not forgive them, they are not forgiven" (John 20:23).

Whoa. It all comes down to this. Jesus left us many critical Kingdom lessons in the final week before his death and resurrection.

He told his disciples, "This is an example of who I am" when he washed their feet.

He showed them, "This is how I love you" when he went to the Cross.

He proclaimed, "This is my peace" when he stood among
  them again.
He breathed on them and said, "This is your mission"
  when he commanded them to forgive.

In these moments, Jesus gave us a gift and a purpose too.
The gift is this new life with the Holy Spirit. And the purpose—the fruit of our life with Christ—is forgiveness. This is
the essence of the gospel—the Good News of Christ. Receiving
and offering forgiveness is your mission too. Receiving and giving grace is your purpose!

Do you know what this means? Do you understand that a
life lived with Christ isn't about doing the big things but doing
these little things?

You see, the disciples were expecting a kingdom. They were
expecting a job title and a position and a clear understanding of
what they had authority over. But instead, the resurrected Jesus
stood among them, breathed on them, and said, "Okay, get out
there and offer forgiveness because that's how people are going
to know me." Talk about a serious perspective change!

Jesus made it clear that the way we live despite the injustices,
the way we heal from the wounds, the way we give grace—that's
evidence of the power of life with him. When we get forgiveness right, we tend to get other parts of our lives right as well,
because a heart full of forgiveness is a heart full of love. Such a
heart is free to experience love and intimacy with Christ in new
ways. It's surrendered to the idea that we need Jesus to wash our
feet; we need him to breathe on us. We need him that close.
Every single day.

So I'll tell you why we forgive. We forgive because Jesus went first. We forgive because Jesus knows the depth of our own sin and our own anger. We forgive because Jesus knows how we've written people off, how we've killed them off in our minds. He knows that we've hurt people when our own hearts have hurt. He knows all of it and yet he still stoops low and washes our feet. He still comes close and breathes on us. He welcomes us joyfully and rejoices when we turn to him. He offers himself with no condition, and we are safe in his embrace. He sees the depth of all you are and all you could be—for better or for worse—and he loves you so much. He gave up all his rights and let himself be beaten and crucified so that we could see that in the spiritual life, the world's way of keeping score is all wrong.

Forgiveness is at the heart of the gospel. So if we don't recognize our anger and don't deal with our hurt, we can't understand forgiveness. Only when we recognize the countless number of times that God has forgiven us will we be brave enough to forgive too. Let's not miss the truth that seeking God's grace and extending God's grace is what we all need more of, in all the day-to-day interactions where anger tends to build.

This kind of forgiveness is what sets us apart as Christians. Giving grace takes courage. It takes grit-your-teeth, white-knuckled courage to decide that you are going to see something differently. That you are going to let someone off the hook. It takes courage to identify hurt, to feel hurt, and to turn that hurt over to God so that he can deal with it.

Just because you've been hurt and wounded doesn't mean it's over. Just because you feel angry and stuck doesn't mean your story has been written. Jesus' last week on earth shows that God is full of surprises, and the story isn't over even when we think the gavel has gone down on the conviction and the last nail has gone into the coffin. God won't be defined by courts or coffins. He doesn't accept our own endings; he makes his own endings. And that's what he can do in your life.

So why forgiveness? Because it's the Jesus way. Because it's what we need more than anything else in this world. And because God's Spirit, living in us, gives us power to forgive others. He makes us do what we can't do on our own. And he doesn't do it because we follow a set of steps. He just changes us as we love him. Because love changes things.

We Let It Happen

The other day I was talking with my friend Megan, who is new in her relationship with Jesus. She's just beginning to use her spiritual survival skills: She's listening to worship music and reading her devotional and trying to soak it all in, but in a lot of ways, she tells me, she still feels the same as she did before. That makes her wonder sometimes if this whole Jesus thing is really sticking.

As we were standing in my kitchen, she told me, "You know what's weird? I'm starting to feel sad for John." John is Megan's stepdad. For as long as I've known Megan, she's hated him. She blamed him for her parents' marriage falling apart. She despised him, and he didn't make himself easy to love. He was rude and mean. He was hurtful to her and to her mom. Every time I was with Megan, she just spewed disgust for him.

So you can imagine how surprised I was when she casually said, "I feel sad for John." I turned from the veggies I was chopping and nearly shouted, *"What?"*

She shrugged. "I don't know what's happening, but when I was thinking about him the other day, I started to feel sorry for him. He's alone, and that made me sad." She let out a nervous little giggle and kept stirring a pot on my stove.

This is the power of Christ in us. We don't muscle our way into thinking or feeling differently. We just let it happen. When Christ's love moves into our hearts, it crowds out the anger and the hurt.

When Christ's love moves into our hearts, it crowds out the anger and the hurt.

We grow in love with Jesus for the grace he's given us. We get acquainted with our own deep need for him. We let out all the hurt and the bad/sad/mad we feel. We realize we are helpless to change anything without him. And then—we just let it happen. We let the Holy Spirit have his way in our hearts. We just stay there—stay in the honesty, stay close to Jesus. We let him come close, and we let him help us let go.

This is the power of the gospel. This is how the world will know that Jesus Christ is stronger than death and that following him means we have the power of life in us—to receive grace for ourselves and to give grace to others. We just have to be brave enough to let God rewrite the story. We have to be brave enough to let him come close, and he'll do the rest.

Brave-Enough Pause

Our Daily Brave

Reflect on this passage from Ephesians 4:30-32 (MSG):

> *Don't grieve God. Don't break his heart. His Holy Spirit, moving and breathing in you, is the most intimate part of your life, making you fit for himself. Don't take such a gift for granted. Make a clean break with all cutting, backbiting,*

profane talk. Be gentle with one another, sensitive. Forgive one another as quickly and thoroughly as God in Christ forgave you.

Read this passage several times. What words or phrases stand out to you?

Pray

Father, you have given me life. You know my weaknesses. You know where I haven't forgiven and where I feel disappointed and stuck. Holy Spirit, breathe life into me. Breathe joy into me. Help me walk into today with power and with purpose.

CHAPTER 6

Brave-Enough Women Don't Fear a Fight

It's worth fighting for. / Baby, sometimes love is war.
AMERICAN YOUNG, "LOVE IS WAR"

ONE OF MY FAMILY's favorite places to go on vacation is Hilton Head, an island off the coast of South Carolina. Dave and I discovered it when our kids were young and fell in love with the wide beaches and calm waters. The ocean waves are gentle, perfect for exploring and wading. Last summer we had the opportunity to visit again. The first day of our trip was exactly as we remembered. We let the water lap our beach chairs as our kids played in the surf. But the next morning, strong winds blew from the south. The gentle ocean became fierce; choppy waves and rogue currents threatened to blow us all into the next state.

I stood at the water's edge and stared toward the horizon.

Though I couldn't see it, a tropical depression had formed hundreds of miles away. At its center, the winds reached 50 mph, a weak storm by hurricane standards. But even a relatively mild disturbance impacted our shore. Despite the great distance between the turbulence and our beach, the ocean was no longer a safe place for us to play.

Storms in our own lives are like that tropical depression. It's easy to underestimate the impact that our own conflicts have on those around us. The tension we carry because of unresolved conflict creates a torque in us that makes it impossible to live in the center of the peace that Jesus offers.

We've been taking brave-enough steps forward together. We've explored what it means to truly follow Jesus, to live out our daily brave, and to embrace true grace for ourselves even as we learn to forgive others. But no matter how much we change, one thing stays true: We are always going to face conflict. We are going to be misunderstood. We are going to feel hurt and confused by some of our relationships. We are going to struggle with family members, old friends, coworkers, and strangers. This relational trouble has the power to derail us from being free, to make us believe and act in ways that aren't led by Jesus. And so here we find yet another category of life in which Jesus offers us his courage so we can break free from dysfunctional patterns of conflict.

I believe every one of us has something in our lives—*right now*—that requires us to engage in conflict. I believe God urgently wants us to learn to fight well; it is a clear mandate for all of us. Throughout the Bible, we are told to prepare for the fight—to hold on to what is true, to work for peace, and to pursue our mission of reconciling the world to Christ.[1]

The Bible also tells us that the main fight of life is "not against flesh and blood" (Ephesians 6:12)—which means that there are spiritual forces that oppose us. We know that faith will require perseverance so we can "fight the good fight" (1 Timothy 6:12). We know that the compelling call of the gospel is to be transformed by it, which means we will need that training we've been talking about throughout our whole journey together. But I think the good Christian girl in all of us wants to believe that we can somehow do all of the above while completely averting trouble.

Think about the last conflict you were in. Did you replay it and try to think about how it could have been prevented in the first place? Remember how we talked about the "fake grace" we offer ourselves in those moments? How freeing it is just to embrace the truth that *trouble is going to happen*. There's nothing we can do to avoid it completely.

In John 16:33, Jesus makes this truth an actual promise! Here we find our Jesus-courage word again: *tharseo*. Jesus tells those who follow him that they should "take heart" (*tharseo*) because he has "overcome the world." But just one breath before that, he makes this promise: "In this world you will have trouble." I split the verse up to avoid missing the first promise that comes before the comforting second one. Here it is again: In this world, you (yes, you!) will have trouble.

We can't avoid conflict, but we can meet Jesus with his *tharseo* power in it. So let's consider how the Holy Spirit strengthens us for conflict and allows us to engage with love, power, and grace. Facing conflict might take an extra dose of brave-enough grit. But this is a place where I'm confident God wants to do great work in your heart. Let's jump in together!

Fighting Words (aka Vacuum-gate)

Dave and I have had a long-standing conflict about the tidiness of our house. The root issue (in addition to the fact that we are two sinful humans) is that our idea of "tidy" is different. We hold different standards about what the house should look like, let's say, on a random Tuesday afternoon. (Sound familiar to anyone?) This difference has led to years of fighting. Years, people. For the first few years, we weren't very advanced in our communication skills, so our fights went something like this:

> Dave stomped around cleaning up.
>
> *Me:* What are you doing?
>
> *Dave:* I'm vacuuming.
>
> *Me (starting to cry):* I just vacuumed. WHY ARE YOU AGAINST ME AND WHY DO YOU CRITICIZE EVERYTHING I DO?

As you can imagine, my sophisticated form of diplomacy fully exceeded Dave's man-brain ability to read the subtle nuances of my needs. As the years have passed, we've learned a lot more about each other. We've learned to give grace and move toward one other in conflict, but we still sometimes see things differently.

When I started working full-time, we shifted from fighting about the tidiness of the house to fighting about the employing of a house cleaner. Considering we had different expectations of what the house should look like, I saw my extra income as a reason to have a house cleaner. It made perfect sense to me. Dave saw my extra income as a reason to start saving for our kids' college funds. It made perfect sense to him.

Holding to our own perspectives makes perfect sense when

we are on our own, but luckily for Dave and me, we've joined forces (and added three kids). Picture our competing expectations as two weather systems slowly moving toward each other—pressure building—and then colliding, in what I like to call the Vacuum-gate scandal.

This is what that looked like one day: I was in the kitchen, frantically trying to pull dinner together after a full day at work. The kids were in various stages of whining, worrying about homework, and shedding and scattering sports equipment, lunch boxes, and school papers faster than I could pick them up. Dave walked in from work and began vacuuming. Now, dear friend, for those of you who are now coveting my husband, for those of you who think that I am now taking my sweet-baby, perfect-angel husband for granted in every way to Sunday, I ask that you extend me enormous grace as I tell you that *I didn't want him to vacuum*. I know. Try to keep reading.

I didn't want him to vacuum because I wanted him to come over, give me a hug, and ask if he could help with dinner. I wanted him to step over the sports equipment and the homework papers because that would feel like love. I wanted him to care about me and my day and come partner with me, not bring his own ideas into how the house should be running. And here's the really honest part—I also felt like him vacuuming was a sign of his disapproval at my ability to keep house, which I squarely felt was my responsibility.

So. That's a lot to feel when you are standing at the sink making dinner. I'd like to say we have grown since our early years of marriage, that my communication has become more gentle and graceful, but that's not always the case. Over the roar of the vacuum, our conversation escalated. And by "conversation," I mean that I was saying lots and lots of words and he was mostly looking down at the carpet. And by "saying," I mean saying loudly. Over the vacuum. So maybe shouting. Okay, for honesty's sake, I was screaming at him over the vacuum cleaner; the storm inside me growing stronger due to the fact that he was

a. ignoring me, or
b. trying to finish vacuuming the rug, or
c. both a and b.

The rest of the evening is a bit of a blur, but I know it included me shouting that I'd rather take a second job selling earrings at the mall to pay for a house cleaner than deal with his unrealistic expectations. Not exactly a shining moment of kindness or gentleness on my part.

Not all of us deal with conflict like this (thank goodness). But all of us deal with it somehow.

We have to understand our default settings in conflict if we are going to grow. The box on page 107 contains a grid that pictures how we handle conflict. On one axis is the *approach*. On the other is the *action*. Let's use my previous example as you explore your own relationship with conflict:

Conflict: The approach

The approach axis describes the way we first handle a confrontation. Most of us have a tendency either to stubbornly ignore or to quickly engage an issue or person we are fighting. On one extreme of the continuum is the *avoider*. This person tends to manage conflict by choosing not to manage it. Even when

Approaches to Conflict

What quadrant do you arc toward?

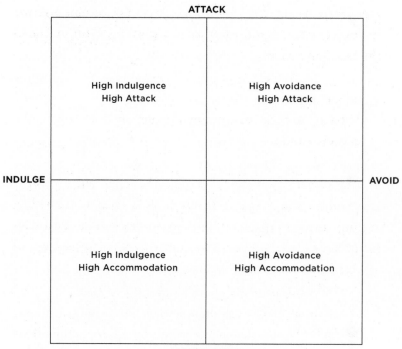

The **Avoider** hates conflict, so her initial approach is to try stopping it before it even starts by ignoring, deflecting, or stuffing her feelings.

The **Indulger** promptly engages with the person or force that opposes her; she is less likely to let go or compromise easily.

The **Accommodator** readily gives up her side of the argument in conflict, even when it's to her detriment. She prefers "keeping the peace" to holding her ground.

The **Attacker** rejects any compromise during conflict. She may turn conflict against the other person and use it as an opportunity to "gain ground" or dominate in a relationship.

things are obviously out of line, an avoider would rather stuff it away, change the topic, or put it off. When a hot topic comes up, an avoider is a master escape artist. Dave's approach was on the avoider side—try to finish vacuuming and pretend that the conflict would go away. If avoidance continues for a long time, people with this tendency may lose touch with their own emotions. It's been so long since they stood up for themselves that they can't decide what actually feels right.

On the other side of the spectrum is the *indulger*. When I say indulgence, you might think of too much dessert. But an indulgent personality is likely to act on impulses with less restraint. When a conflict comes up, the indulger sees that action is necessary. She is willing to engage the problem head-on but might see others as her adversaries and have a harder time choosing to let something go. My approach to the vacuuming argument was on the indulgent side—let's have it out.

Our avoidant or indulgent approach represents our typical attitude as we approach a conflict.

We are all somewhere on the spectrum, and our avoidant or indulgent approach represents our typical attitude as we *approach* a conflict. Eventually, though, the pressure systems of conflict come to a head. The action axis describes what we do when we are actually *in* the conflict.

Conflict: The action

Once forced into conflict, we tend to act in one of two ways: accommodate or attack. *Accommodators* are on one side of the spectrum and tend to give up the fight quickly. Their action is inaction, choosing not to fight by surrendering all to the other person or force in life that is opposing them.

On the other end of the axis is the *attacker*. Once the conflict begins, the attacker becomes like the Alamo, refusing to give up even one inch of her ground or turning the conflict around as a chance to take ground from the other. Attackers who initially approach conflict by trying to avoid it will eventually explode. For example, during a spat with a teenager about picking up clothes off the floor, an attacker might lob this accusation: "You leave your clothes on the floor because you don't listen to a word I say, and you disrespect everything I try to do around here!"

Where would you plot yourself on this chart? What is your "default mode" in conflict?

Biblical Fights

Let's look at a few case studies from Scripture to see how people handle conflict—and how God handles his people. Take the prophet Jonah. If we were to plot Jonah on our conflict scale, we'd probably place him in the high avoidance/high attack quadrant. When faced with the choice to obey God's clear command for his life, Jonah chose to run (that's avoidance). As the story developed, Jonah appeared to go into accommodation mode, pledging to be obedient to God and do what he said. But after Jonah went to Nineveh to preach truth, as God instructed him to do, his true relationship with conflict was revealed. In the scorching Middle Eastern sun, Jonah fired back, complaining to God about his decisions and continuing to defend Jonah's own reasons for running in the first place. That's attack mode. Even though Jonah's behavior fell in line, his heart didn't.

We operate this way when we follow God's commands with our actions but keep our hearts far away from him. This incongruence between our inside and our outside is exhausting. To "keep up an act" with anyone—our husbands, our kids, our boss, or our God—is entirely consuming. The deception of avoidance or accommodating is that it makes us feel like we are doing the right thing—acting like good Christians. But inside of us, a pressure system is building. And that pressure requires action: Sometimes bad behavior needs to be confronted. Sometimes bad behavior requires us to work through forgiveness and understanding. So even when avoiding or accommodating is the "right thing," it can be destructive if our hearts are far from love.

One of the greatest indicators that we've closed our hearts when dealing with a difficult relationship is a comprehensive lack of joy.

How do we know if this describes us in conflict? I find that one of the greatest indicators that we've closed our hearts when dealing with a difficult relationship is a comprehensive lack of joy that impacts much more than just the situation we are in. In all spheres of life, we begin to notice that our hearts are becoming embittered and hard. This is a spiritual 911 situation that we'll talk about a little later.

Let's move forward into the New Testament and examine the life of Peter. The accounts of Peter put his tendencies in the high indulgence/high attack quadrant of our scale. As Jesus was being arrested, Peter whipped out a sword and cut off the ear of the servant to the high priest.[2] Later, when confronted by a bystander about his allegiance to Jesus, Peter denied it "with an oath" (Matthew 26:72), or as my "Nicole translation" might put it: "He cursed him out." Peter gives us a great example of how stress tends to reveal our true nature. In his case, it manifested itself in a quick temper and impulsive action. Throughout the Gospels, we see that Peter knew what it meant to give in to the temptation of sin. In fact, in the biblical account of Jesus' arrest and crucifixion, we see Peter's courage melting, his resolve fading, and his will turning from the truth.

About thirty years after this soul-defining week in Peter's life, he penned a letter to the emerging Christian churches that he had helped establish. In one of those letters, he warned the church, "Be alert and of sober mind. Your enemy the devil prowls around like a roaring lion looking for someone to devour" (1 Peter 5:8). I think Peter knew what it felt like to be consumed by anger and self-protection, to be tempted to handle our fights ourselves rather than turning and choosing God's way. But Peter also knew the sweet relief of forgiveness and reconciliation. He knew personally his own need for grace, and it changed him completely. His letters reflect a man who knew what it meant to lose it—lose his will, lose his courage, lose his temper—and yet to be reconciled back into a whole new life through Christ.

Scripture also includes examples of people on the high avoidance/high accommodation side of the conflict spectrum. In 1 and 2 Kings, we read about leaders of Israel who chose to accommodate the culture, avoiding the inevitable clashes they would face if they led their people by God's commands. Isaiah 30:1 speaks to this time: "'What sorrow awaits my rebellious children,' says the LORD. 'You make plans that are contrary to mine. You make alliances not directed by my Spirit, thus piling up your sins'" (NLT).

King Solomon was given all the riches and wisdom of the world (see 2 Chronicles 1:12), but his inability to fight off the winds of the culture and his own desires led him into disobedience and broke his full devotion to God (see 1 Kings 11). Sometimes he and other kings made deliberate choices toward evil, but many times they seemed to fall into evil by choosing *not* to fight. A treaty might seem like a good idea—except when it's not God's idea. Our own ways of keeping peace may seem right—except when God has something better planned.

All of us, too, fall in various places on this conflict quadrant. Perhaps we are like Solomon, wise in many things but weak in certain areas. We may handle conflict well at work but terribly with our husband. Some of us are like Peter—what you see is what you get, and sometimes our actions move faster than our self-control. Some of us are like Jonah—we avoid conflict by ignoring and running in our hearts, and even when we seem to submit to God's will, our hearts may be far from him.

We also need to take all of Scripture into account when trying to discern how to deal with conflict. That's because the Bible talks about lots of different ways to handle it. First Peter 4:8 seems to indicate we should accommodate others: "Love covers over a multitude of sins." Luke 17:3 says to confront wrong: "If your brother or sister sins against you, rebuke them." Matthew 5:39 seems to encourage avoidance: "Do not resist an evil person. If anyone slaps you on the right cheek, turn to them the other cheek also." Titus 1:9 teaches leaders to "refute those who oppose [sound doctrine]": that sounds like a reason to attack. No wonder we have a hard time knowing how to fight correctly—how to find the balance between confronting and ignoring, between holding our ground and letting go.

When taken as a whole, these verses show us the truth about resolving conflict effectively: If we insist on taking only one approach to all disagreements, we may be missing the bigger picture. If we are fully tipped toward the avoidant side, we are likely to abandon honesty. If we are fully tipped toward the indulgent side, we are likely to abandon self-control.

Scripture teaches us that to deal with conflict well, we sometimes need to live in the middle—letting go at times, facing the fight in others.

Jesus: Perfect Balance

Deciding the best way to deal with conflict may not always be easy, but we can look to one person who always got it right. What if we plotted Jesus on our scale? Of course, we know he belongs right in the center—he was our perfect example of how to live on the earth, and he continues to be our teacher as we learn from him. We know that in theory, but I think in practice, most of us think of Jesus as meek and mild, far over on the avoidance/accommodation side of the grid. But Jesus did and said many things that aren't exactly Pinterest-worthy.

To deal with conflict well, we sometimes need to live in the middle—letting go at times, facing the fight in others.

When was the last time you saw one of these stories shared on someone's social media as an encouragement from the life of Jesus?

- Jesus made a whip and drove everyone out of the Temple courts. He sent the animals on their way, slapped coins around, and overturned the vendors' tables. He looked at those selling sacrifices and said, "Get these out of here!" (see John 2:15-16). *That's not exactly the mild-mannered Jesus we may sometimes picture.*

- When Jesus told his disciples about his upcoming suffering and death, Peter took him aside to rebuke him. Jesus looked at him and said, "Get behind me, Satan! You are a stumbling block to me" (Matthew 16:23). *Not exactly meek.*

- When Jesus' mother and brothers came to take charge of him because they thought he was out of his mind, Jesus refused to go out to talk with them, saying, "Whoever does God's will is my brother and sister and mother" (see Mark 3:21-35). *Not exactly gentle.*

- When the disciples suggested calling fire down from heaven against a Samaritan town that didn't welcome them, Jesus rebuked them sharply (see Luke 9:55). The Greek word used here, *epitimao*, describes confronting people and forces with strength. *It sounds to me like Jesus told them to shut up.*

The Bible calls Jesus "the Lion of the tribe of Judah" (Revelation 5:5). Lions are sleek *and* tough. Lions are beautiful *and* strong. Lions might lie quietly, but they roar loudly. Jesus is humble and meek, but there are times when Jesus stands up for the fight. He gets angry. He ignores his mother when she opposes him. He rebukes and corrects his loved ones and his friends. This is the Jesus we may be less familiar with, and if we don't know the aspects of Jesus' strength in conflict, we may continue to believe that the only way to be a peacemaker is to never fight for what's right. We can easily interpret the stories we've heard and the feelings we've felt to mean that conflict-avoidant is the way to go, that it's never worth fighting about anything. But I hope this brief survey of the other side of Jesus proves that's not the way Jesus lived it.

So what about the "tender and mild" Jesus?[3] When Judas, Jesus' follower and disciple, betrayed him, Jesus looked at him and said, "Do what you came for, friend" (Matthew 26:50). Before Judas and a large crowd of chief priests and elders thirsty for a fight, Jesus simply let events happen. We know that Jesus didn't defend himself in front of the Sanhedrin or in front of Pilate. He didn't appeal to the crowd when they yelled, "Crucify him!" He went quietly to his death.

Can you imagine being in that crowd, perhaps as one of the people who saw Jesus call Lazarus out from the tomb after he had been dead four days? Can you imagine now seeing him as he appeared—weak, powerless, and undefended? Our Messiah was as Scripture foretold: "He was oppressed and afflicted, yet he did not open his mouth; he was led like a lamb to the slaughter, and as a sheep before its shearers is silent, so he did not open his mouth" (Isaiah 53:7). During his arrest, trial, and crucifixion, we do see another side of Jesus. We see the side that was willing to suffer unto death because he knew he was on the path his Father had put him on.

The Common Denominator: Obedience

So Jesus sometimes fought, and sometimes he relented. We know that he was always under control even when he was turning tables over. But let's face it: Conflict is hard, and it's even harder when we don't know when to fight and when to let go. What can we learn from Jesus' perfect approach? Here are three questions to ask ourselves when we think about conflict in our lives:

1. *How much of me is in this?* Remember the let-it-all-out exercise in the last chapter? That is designed to get us to a place of honesty. A friend of mine was telling me about a recent conflict with her husband. At one point, she lowered her voice to say, "Sometimes his mere presence bothers me." Okay, that's honest! When we face a conflict, we need to know how much of "me" is in it. If I'm bothered because my husband is merely standing in my way when I'm trying to unload the dishwasher, there's a whole lot of me in that.

    I think those prickly little conflicts are opportunities for us to become really familiar with our own shortcomings—to walk away for a moment and ask God to restore our love for that person. It's okay sometimes to not like the people you love. And praise be to God—he can make you like them again. Sometimes there's a lot more "me" in a conflict than is healthy or helpful. And when that's the case, we need God's intervention before anything good will come from a confrontation.

    When someone bothers us, angers us, or disappoints us, we must start by shining the light on our own hearts. Stopping to ask God to help reveal our motivations is a step toward healthy conflict. Why are we acting or reacting a certain way? Have we been giving ourselves to a person because of what we expected back? Have we given up our own rights because we are waiting for someone to become who we want them to be? If so, we are acting out of our own needs rather than out of selfless motivation—*even though those two motivations might look the same on the outside.*

True—our motivations may never be perfectly pure.
But when we deceive ourselves into thinking that there
isn't any "me" in our conflict, we are headed for trouble.
I once accidently told a huge group of women, "No one
likes perfect women." Ironically, I was being very imper-
fect at the moment, as my mouth got ahead of my words.
However, the moment sticks with me, mostly because I
think it's true.

One of the greatest gifts we give
those around us is an accurate sense
of our weaknesses. Those limits
and failures aren't a reason to give
up or never stand up for ourselves.
Instead, our limits humble us to
approach conflict with love and gentleness rather than
with salt and vinegar, to assume that we have as many
issues as the person we are confronting. There is grace
and courage in that approach.

> *When we deceive our-
> selves into thinking that
> there isn't any "me"
> in our conflict, we are
> headed for trouble.*

2. *What am I fighting for? What do I hope will happen
   from this fight? Do I have a sense of what I want?* If our
   best answer for why we are confronting someone is
   "because," we may want to think more about it. In a
   marriage class at my church, our pastor teaches about
   the goals of conflict. In marriage, he says, the goal
   of conflict should always be oneness. We sometimes
   have to fight so we can get back on the same page. We
   sometimes have to confront so that we can ask for forgiveness and change the ways we are talking, thinking,
   or acting toward a person.

   A great reason for fighting is to restore unity. We

don't fight to get our way, get our due, or get revenge.
The Bible points us toward restoration and reconciliation in relationships—not toward our rights. When
was the last time you approached a conflict with
someone with the desire to understand him or her?
So often when we are mad and hurt, we want to react
because *we* need to be understood. We don't truly want
to understand or hear the other person.

When a relationship is consistently rocky, it
might be time to turn the focus on ourselves. We
might ask, *Is there something in me—even unin-
tentional—that might be making this relationship
difficult? Is there a pattern in me (like where I fall on
the conflict grid) that's creating difficulty in multiple
relationships?*

The painful truth of conflict is that sometimes
we want more than a person can give. Sometimes we
have an expectation of what a loved one can be and
do for us that exceeds his or her actual capacity. This
is hard because we feel our intentions are pure—and
they might be. We may feel that we are giving far
more to the relationship than the person is offering
in return. Of course, that's disappointing and hard.
But we have an opportunity to be brave in our disappointment. Rather than following the same well-worn
patterns in our hearts, we can turn in another direction.
Because of the loving relationship we enjoy with the
Trinity—Father, Son, and Holy Spirit—we can bring
this sadness to God. In our disappointment, we can ask
for God's help in understanding our own motivation

within this relationship. What do we expect from this person? Why do we expect it? Our prayer might sound something like this:

> *Father in heaven, I am so disappointed in my relationship with _____. I expected her to be more available to me in this challenging time. I expected her to care for me when I called her last week, but it feels like she just shrugged me off. I guess I expected more out of her. I thought she would care for me because we have such a long friendship and I've done so much for her. Please help me to view this situation, and this person, through your eyes.*

These words will be familiar territory to Jesus. He knows what it's like to have your family disregard you and your friends desert you. Jesus knows what it's like to feel abandoned and alone. He can identify with your condition—and even more, he can strengthen you to handle it. Ephesians 3:16 says that God the Father can "strengthen you with power through his Spirit in your inner being." We worship and then we pray. In that inner stillness we commune with the Spirit, who comforts and strengthens us. We allow his courage to infuse us, and then we face our conflict head-on. We admit with accuracy what we are expecting and why we are expecting it. And then we turn to Jesus.

3. *Am I being obedient?* The one consistent thread throughout Jesus' life was his unrelenting, uncompromising

obedience to his Father. In John 8:28, Jesus said, "I do nothing on my own." Nothing. He was always perfectly aligned with his heavenly Father and empowered by the Holy Spirit. When Jesus whipped those tables over, he did it from obedience. When Jesus stood silently as he was beaten, mocked, and cursed, he did it from obedience. Jesus listened for and acted on that direction, never rushing ahead or lagging behind his Father's perfect plan—even when that plan looked like disaster and defeat.

What would our lives be like if we followed Jesus' example for even one day? The offer of life in Christ is the offer to live in this kind of relationship aligned with the Father. We practice our spiritual survival skills daily so that we, too, can listen, receive, and act on the direction of our heavenly Father. In communion with the Trinity, we never have to feel alone in a decision or confused in a conflict.

It takes great courage to wait in silence and surrender for God's words. I have found in my life that confusion in a conflict is an invitation from God to seek him first, to wait on him, and to continue searching the Scripture for a promise or a comfort or a challenge that addresses my situation. I am constantly reminded that God is much more patient than I am, especially in the murky waters of conflict. But he has always shown up for me there, even if it wasn't in my timing. Meanwhile, you can be sure that God has not forgotten you: "Wait for the Lord; be strong and take heart and wait for the Lord" (Psalm 27:14).

God has promised that he will be with us. He promises repeatedly that he will give us direction. Proverbs 3:6 tells us that if in all ways we acknowledge God, he will direct our paths. "All ways" certainly includes the little and big actions we take in relationships. Isaiah 30 promises that when we wait for God, when we cry out for help from him, he will respond: "Whether you turn to the right or to the left, your ears will hear a voice behind you, saying, 'This is the way; walk in it'" (verse 21). Moreover, Jesus calls himself "the way" (John 14:6).

Maybe more than anything, we need to know that there is a way forward, that God makes a way, and that Jesus models the way. No matter what crisis you find yourself in, no matter how far gone it feels that your relationship is, God has a way. His way may lead you to confront or to forgive, to reconcile or to walk away. But there is an answer, my friend. There is a way to be obedient in it and through it. It may start with an honest prayer, admitting you've given up on things ever being better. It may begin with your heart releasing the situation or the person over to God's loving hands. Let him hold your concerns for a while. You keep seeking him and keep practicing your spiritual survival skills, and he'll send the situation back your way when the time is right.

It's okay to wait on the Lord. It's okay to cry out to him—not one time, but as many times as it takes for you to get the "you" out of that conflict, for you to get really honest about what you want, and for you to receive God's direction for your life. Once you've surrendered your life to his guidance, Jesus might not act as quickly as you'd like—after all, he won't be rebuked or domesticated. But don't give up. Don't stop seeking. Don't stop going to the Lord with those places of hurt and bitterness and laying them at his feet. Let him act on your behalf and let him lead you. He'll do it—directing you to one small step of obedience at a time, giving you the opportunity to follow his way. It may feel like defeat or even a small death to you as you go. But know that the ultimate destination is "life . . . to the full" (John 10:10).

Courage in Conviction

As I've said before, it is in the small, sticky situations in our everyday lives that we most often have opportunities to be brave enough to be different. Case in point: I have a friend whose husband's passion for fantasy football borders on obsession. I can say that because he's not my husband and I don't have to deal with his drafts, leagues, and endless discussions over trades and his incredibly strong feelings about make-believe teams. My friend and I were recently laughing about— I mean, discussing—this "hobby" and her struggle to take it seriously. This is where the conversation actually turned to faith (believe it or not). As we were talking, my friend said to me, "Well, it was hard, but I said to him this morning, 'I want you to have a great draft tonight, honey. How can I support you?'"

Even when she repeated the words to me it sounded like she was choking. But she actually did mean them! Because she loves her husband, because she supports him, because she made a vow to be "in it" with him—in the stumbling forward movement of life, in jobs, children, chores, and dreams, and in football season and out of season—she allowed the Holy Spirit to give her *conviction* about how to love her husband well in that moment.

Conviction takes two forms in our spiritual life. The first kind of conviction is the exposure of our guilt. In John 16:8, Jesus promises that the Holy Spirit's main job will be to "convict the world regarding sin and righteousness and judgment" (NASB). The Holy Spirit is a convincer and a "convicter." He testifies to truth. The Holy Spirit helps us to see the other side of the story, so that while we are laughing about fantasy football, he's right there, gently reminding our inner being that *love is patient* (1 Corinthians 13:4), gently telling us that *greater love has no one than this, that one lay down his life for his friends* (John 15:13). You may ignore his voice, but he's a persistent presence, with more words, like *let us make every effort to do what leads to peace and mutual edification* (Romans 14:19) and *we love because he first loved us* (1 John 4:19).

We may fight it off for a while, with a *Really, God? Really? Fantasy football?* But he sticks with us, shedding light on our own selfishness, reminding us that we, too, are sometimes hard to love. Conviction is God turning on the light in the dirty corners of our own soul. Conviction is God's white-glove inspection of our own hearts that leads us to repentance. The Holy Spirit convicts us of our sin and reminds us of our lack of righteousness outside of God's incredible grace. He reminds us that we love only because he first loved us. Conviction softens us, like God's strong hands unknotting the taut fibers of sin around our hearts. For my friend, conviction is what reminds her that she loves her husband enough to actually care about fantasy football—merely because he cares about it.

> Conviction softens us, like God's strong hands unknotting the taut fibers of sin around our hearts.

The second form of conviction is the commitment to become more like Christ in our life. When we are brave enough to do the work we are talking about in this book, we are digging down deep, setting a solid foundation about who we are and what's worth fighting for. True convictions have power and depth. It is not my friend's conviction of the worth of fantasy football that motivates her actions. It is her deep conviction about love.

So often we hang out in the shallower places of our souls, in the place of circumstances and the daily storm of our emotional ups and downs. Instead of fighting to get past the initial breaker waves of whatever is slowing us down—fantasy football, the minor annoyances of life, our own insecurities—we just give up and resign ourselves to the shallow. We let relationships erode, one petty argument at a time, because we don't want or don't know how to get deeper.

But this is where the Holy Spirit works once again. First Thessalonians 1:5 says that the gospel of Jesus Christ comes with "power, with the Holy Spirit and deep conviction." Surrendering our lives to Jesus is the fuel. The Holy Spirit starts the engine. And we are propelled into the deeper places where we find the passion and conviction to conduct ourselves with grace and truth.

So conviction is what informs our daily interactions, whether with the stranger at the grocery store, with our coworkers and acquaintances, or with our closest family members and friends. Conviction of our own sin keeps us soft with others. Conviction of the beliefs worth fighting for keeps us firm in the storm and draws us into deeper places—it grows us into maturity, so that we can be an anchor of truth and hope for this world.

When Life Is Really Hard

Since I used a marriage story, I have to address what I know is going on with some of you, dear sisters. You may be thinking, *My marriage is too far gone.* Or *If you knew my story, you would know that what God is asking for is impossible.* Some of you are wishing that the worst arguments you had with your husband were about fantasy football. You have deep brokenness and wounds in your story. Your relationship with your spouse or a family member or a former friend feels so painful that you are sick over it. Your conviction—your deep-seated belief about the sheer hopelessness of the situation—feels cemented around your heart.

Being in ministry allows me to enter into many women's stories, and I know there is pain that feels like a deep ravine that can never be crossed. There are so many difficult ways our relationships fracture. There are complicated dynamics that go back generations—deep turbulence caused by fear, sin, and pain that ripple out into our relationships and marriages. But love is worth fighting for. Even if the misunderstandings and distance go back months or years, even if you feel so far gone you don't think you can make your way back, remember that God can make a way. He is an expert guide in heart navigation, and he is willing to be in this hard place with you.

You can begin by admitting that you feel lost and committing to spend time every day in God's presence, opening your heart to where he is leading you in this struggle. If your conflict is in your marriage, you can start by offering your husband a gift that he doesn't even know he's getting. You can devote five minutes of your day to praying for him. This is between you and God. This is not for you to use in your next argument with him, as in "I've been praying for you every day, and you can't even put your socks away?" This will defeat the purpose.

Vow to keep this prayer commitment a secret. Your husband may not seem spiritually in tune—he may not even know God. But you can still bring him into God's presence every day, and let God chart a course. Try it for a month. Try it for two. Commit to it and tell one friend about it, a friend who can ask you if you are sticking with it. Be accountable to a month of God's presence, and be open to wherever God would lead and convict you. You took vows with this man in front of God to fight for it—to fight for marriage. So even if you can't muster up the feelings to do it for your man, do it for your God. He's done greater miracles than this, and he can do them in your soul.

At times, though, relationships break and stay broken. There are husbands who walk away. There are a million little steps traveled between "I do" and an affair. Or addiction. Or abandonment. Or abuse. And as much as I wish it weren't true, I know that some marriages will not be repaired. There is nothing—not one thing—that God cannot redeem and overcome. He can restore your heart and your marriage, or he can restore your heart and not your marriage. But he will restore you, no matter what. He will redeem the worst pain. He will heal the deepest wounds. Sometimes that comes with the full restoration of relationship, and sometimes it doesn't.

One of my closest friends went through a necessary but painful divorce recently. She called on the Lord, who strengthened her for the battle. But after months of prayer, after counseling, after trying and trying again—reconciliation didn't come.

Although she held out hope that her husband could change, that's not what happened. It was the worst thing she's ever experienced, but she was able to endure the hardship, to continue to be a brave-enough mom to her young children, and to lean into Jesus even in what could not be explained and what will not be restored. It is trite but it is also true—she is stronger now. Although the grounds for her divorce stemmed from her husband's actions, she also had the courage to face her own weaknesses in the midst of it. She went through months of counseling to face her own issues. She uprooted some deeply held convictions that were not from God. And she planted some new beliefs of her worth, her dignity, and her loveliness that are as true as gravity.

This is the incredible, miraculous, restoring work of the Spirit. These are some of the unexpected and transformative places that facing conflict can take us. We can be brave enough for this. It starts with understanding what we bring to our relationships. It leads us to deeper places of truth with Christ. And then he wonderfully, gently, lovingly carries us forward—to speak up, to be silent, to say yes, and to say no. First Timothy 4:10 says, "We labor and strive, because we have put our hope in the living God."

I imagine we all have some work and even some suffering to do when it comes to handling conflict. But we do it so that we can be led to the truth, and we do it because it brings truth to others. We place our hope squarely in the living God, the one who promises to guide us into all truth, to strengthen us in the most difficult of circumstances, and to bring healing into our own hearts and into our relationships as we face these fights.

Brave-Enough Pause

Look at the conflict grid on page 107. Consider a few of your closest relationships. Where would you plot yourself on the grid when considering the way you handle conflict with each person? If you are feeling particularly brave, ask your spouse or a close friend how he or she sees you handling conflict.

Our Daily Brave

In what ways do your patterns in conflict feel unhealthy? What's one thing you'd like to do differently in one of those close relationships?

Consider the following statements of Jesus:

> *God blesses those who work for peace, for they will be called the children of God.*
> **Matthew 5:9,** NLT
>
> *Love your enemies! Pray for those who persecute you!*
> **Matthew 5:44,** NLT

Are you willing to commit to pray for an adversary for a period of time? Can you find a partner to be accountable to during this time?

Pray

Father, I feel the tension and emotion of conflict in my life. Would you unknot the cords of conflict from my soul and give me the courage to follow your gentle pull toward a life of true peace? I open my heart to your guidance, your conviction, and the ways you want to change me through the conflicts I'm experiencing right now.

CHAPTER 7

Brave-Enough Women Explore Their Territory

I always wanted to be somebody, but now I
realize I should have been more specific.

LILY TOMLIN

MY DAUGHTER HAS A THING for shoes, and she comes by it naturally. When Cameron was just five days old, I tucked her in a sling as I shopped the clearance section of Old Navy. We've spent many moments together in the shoe aisle since that day nine years ago. This generational pattern yields both adorable shoes and also some self-control issues.

A few weeks ago Cameron was amusing herself with one of her favorite activities—wearing my shoes. She buckled on a pair of high-heeled sandals and began a confident march around my room. "Mom, how old do I have to be to wear high heels?" she asked me for the thirteenth time in a week.

I did not have an answer for her, so I dodged her question yet again by answering, "I don't know when, but *not now*."

She sighed dramatically while changing into another pair. "I can't wait to be *older*," she said, pausing over a particularly glittery wedge. "All the good stuff is for *women*."

Cameron's foray into fashion isn't just about fashion. She is thinking about her future. She's dreaming about what she will be like when she grows up. She's imagining who she can be. And as I watch her watching the world, I begin to dream with her too. Because the question in her heart—*Who will I become?*—isn't just for little girls. It's a question for all of us, and answering it takes great courage.

We've been talking about being brave enough—brave enough to live the life God has given us. But now we will talk about being brave enough to live beyond that—to live out our calling. To be brave enough for this, we need everything we've learned up to this point. So far, we've been addressing some foundational if/then truths you'll need for your inner life:

If you're a student of Jesus, *then* you have to commit
    to and practice following him daily.
If you're living in true grace, *then* the way you think, act,
    and feel will be different.
If you're giving that true grace, *then* your life and mission
    will be marked by forgiveness.
If you're defined by that grace and forgiveness, *then* you
    will approach conflict differently.

All of these if/then statements represent the needs that must be met so that you have the courage to flourish into your full self. In order to be confident and courageous, your understanding of grace, forgiveness, and conflict must be rooted in Christ. Out of this foundation of love, you can become a woman of purpose and freedom.

So now we turn to the question each of us must answer: *Who am I becoming?* This question has confounded, confused, and thrilled me for most of my life. It's a question that requires you and me to pull back the layers of task and circumstance that often define our daily lives. It requires each of us to bring our whole heart—what our life tells us, what our hopes and passions and skills tell us—and be willing to let that whole truth inform what God is beckoning us toward. Many of us go our whole lives avoiding or ignoring the question of who we are becoming, choosing to settle for good enough instead of brave enough.

Yet God has designed a world in which his children were created to shine brightly and to do their part to make the body of Christ as healthy and vibrant and effective as it can be.[1] Your life, right now, is begging you to discover the person you are meant to be. The murmurings of your heart that wonder if life has purpose and meaning, those little internal whispers telling you that *there must be more than this* . . . those are some of the truest voices in you.

Many of us choose to settle for good enough instead of brave enough.

If you can drum up the courage to look for your purpose, if you can cease your daily nonstop activities for just a moment, I think you'll discover a beautiful, unexpected adventure. The question *Who am I becoming?* takes all kinds of forms. It can sound like this:

What am I good at?
How am I wired?

What are my gifts?

How can I be used in God's Kingdom?

When we are brave enough to seek the answers to these questions, our lives have meaning. Like a compass that provides direction, our sense of who we are and why we are here gives our hearts the ability to filter out the less-than-optimal opportunities and relationships. That soul compass, the understanding of our calling, keeps us from getting off course. When we have a sense of who we are meant to be, we are less likely to try to be someone else.

When we have a sense of who we are meant to be, we are less likely to try to be someone else.

Conversely, when we don't know who we are becoming, our lives feel reactive. Rather than growing into maturity, into strength and power and purpose, we remain directionless and allow our lives and calendars to control us. Our lives may start feeling like a train with no brakes that has derailed and is hurtling us toward an abyss of never-ending obligations, to-do lists, and responsibilities.

So if discovering our purpose gives our lives direction and meaning, why don't more of us do it? And why does it take courage to uncover it anyway? Simply put, many things that are beautiful are hard to come by. Many things worth doing are very hard to do. It is a beautiful and worthy venture to become the woman God created you to be. But it's not easy.

Women = Complicated

I think one reason we may find it hard to answer the question "Who am I becoming?" is because we women are the most complicated creatures on earth. Not only are we intricately wired—a jumble of thoughts, emotions, dreams, and stories—but often our circumstances are complicated. Take my friend Sarah. She is an attorney whose husband recently deployed on a ship with the Navy for three months. She has three boys. The youngest is three. She's also juggling a move across the state, a house renovation, a new nanny, and an ailing mother.

Even though it's tiring, Sarah loves her life. She loves her job. She loves her boys. Life is good, but it is complicated. Sometimes our circumstances give us lots of choices—we are educated, we are valued at work and at home, but we still have to ask the question: *What is the best me that I can offer the world?*

Choices are complicated for younger women too. Take my friend Olivia. She's a twenty-year-old single mom who is trying to finish college. She's balancing the smack-in-the-face surprise of motherhood as she navigates Medicaid, day care, pediatrician appointments—and Econ 201. Life is moving fast, and Olivia is living a life that she never expected. Her life is less about choices and more about survival, but even with a completely unexpected calling in this young season of life, Olivia faces the big question of her future: "What does life hold for me?"

Whether you are a college student or a single mom, pursuing a career or pursuing home schooling, you have to face the same questions as every other woman. In the season you are in, with the circumstances you face, what does God have for you? Who are you meant to be?

Women = Confused

Several years ago, I explored the question, "What is a modern woman?" I asked Facebook friends. I polled women on the streets.

I recorded their answers and compared them to social psychology studies about women's happiness. And what emerged from that exploration were some simple truths about what it's like to figure out womanhood, and they still resonate with me. Which of these statements sound like you?

"A modern woman is self-confident, while all the time she doesn't know who that self is."

"A modern woman is independent to a fault."

"A modern woman tries to be all things to all people."

Underneath all of the answers, there was one common beat. "Independent. Multitasker." *Independent. Multitasker. Independent. Multitasker. Independent. Multitasker.*

I can do it all. I can do it all myself.

And we wonder why we are so tired?

The relationships, the obligations, the needs of those around us can be overwhelming. Like a child lost in a department store, we can find ourselves wandering, not sure if we are headed in the right direction. And because our lives can feel so demanding, it's hard to do more than just react. But there is more for you. There is more for me. There is a God who calls us the "children of the light," who calls us "out of darkness into his wonderful light" (see 1 Thessalonians 5:5 and 1 Peter 2:9). We do not have to live in confusion.

But here's the catch: God isn't going to give us a detailed job description for our lives. He's not going to show us all the steps in the journey—that wouldn't take faith, would it? So he won't show us every step, but he will show us the next step. He does promise to lead. And he does have a specific purpose for each of us.

Women = Called

No two words describe my own journey into my calling more than *complicated* and *confused*. For years, I was so unsure and disturbed about my life's purpose that I avoided the question altogether. I just floated for a while—different jobs, different friend groups, different pet projects. I looked with envy on the women who had lives I wanted. I looked up to the leaders and the teachers of the world, believing they had some kind of X factor that was given out in some class I missed. I believed that not everyone is wired for a passionate purpose and a clear sense of direction. I just decided that they were haves and I was a have-not.

Life was good and full of all the things that I thought were enough—I enjoyed what I was doing, I was having kids, and I was helping out at church. Life was so full of "good enough" that it seemed presumptuous to think I needed more. I still felt a vague dissatisfaction within myself, but I didn't talk about it with anyone. I didn't even think I had the right to keep bringing my frustration to God. I decided that those long-ignored dreams of who he might have made me to be were best left ignored. But—I just couldn't shake the feeling that there must be something more.

The definition of *serendipity* is the "the faculty or phenomenon of finding valuable or agreeable things not sought for."[2] My secondary definition of serendipity is, "There is a good God who's seeking after you with great affection." Through a series of serendipitous events, none of which I planned, I ended up attending a conference women in ministry, which set in motion a series of events over the next several years.

For me, it started with small steps of obedience. I had a desire to help women know how to read and study the Bible and feel like it truly applied to their lives. So I took little risks. I taught at women's groups when I was asked. Then I decided to write homework to expand on the teaching. I helped lead a women's group at my home church, Hope Church, but I also said yes to other volunteer leadership opportunities, from one-on-one counseling with people to helping with a capital campaign.

These doors of opportunity were not ones that I created or forced myself into—though to be honest, I did attempt that approach at times. But whenever I tried to get God to hurry up, to force his hand, and to advocate and angle with him for what I thought I wanted, God kept bringing me back to the small steps of obedience. He used my frustrations and stalled-out seasons to refine my passion, to help me know when I was seeking my own glory instead of his, and to help me realize that the small acts of obedience were more important to him than worldly success.

God taught me to explore my calling in small ways—such as by teaching my children, engaging in one-on-one relationships, and leading small groups—before he opened the door to other things—retreats, books, leadership positions. Now that I'm in full-time ministry at Hope Church, a place that has encouraged me to use my gifts of teaching and leading, I'm amazed. I never would have chosen God's timeline or God's way of refining my passion. But I can look back on it now and call it *good*.

Those years of struggle, obedience, questioning, and waiting taught me that when you seek a life purpose—a calling, if you will—you are not asking for too much. That season taught me that you can never be too old to find what God has for you. And they made me passionate about wanting women to know that not one shred of their stories is wasted when they're devoted to God's glory. When we commit our whole hearts to him and what he's passionate about, I believe he gives his whole heart back to us. And *believing that* is the beginning of your calling.

What Is a Calling Anyway?

The idea of a calling comes from the same root word as *vocation*. Vocation has the Latin root for "voice" in it and is defined as a strong impulse toward a particular activity or career or "a function or station in life to which one is called by God."[3] So the idea of vocation means something beyond a job or role, something that transcends circumstances and has more to do with the particular "call" that awakens the deepest and most real part of us.

I always assumed that with a calling would come a career. I think somewhere in the deeper parts of myself I believed that what God would call me to would also align with what the world would call success. Because of that deep belief, I kept missing his voice, filtering out experiences that I assumed were unimportant and straining on toward some perfect job or title or position that would fill these voids in me. And when I began to have children, it only got worse. Now I felt that God had placed me in a wrestling hold that meant I would never see a calling through. But it was in those years of life with babies and toddlers that he gently, persistently showed me that calling may or may not have anything to do with a career. It was in those dry years of my soul that I began to learn what it means to have a calling and to live it out.

Your calling is the place where your wiring and gifts align with God's expression of love to the world.

Looking back at that time, I would give this simple definition of a calling:

> The place where your wiring and gifts align with God's expression of love to the world.[4]

Imagine your calling as a prism. God is the source of light, and when his light hits that prism just right, it erupts in a glorious rainbow of color. A prism without the light is pretty enough, but when the light hits it, it comes alive. Calling is that intersection where God's light illuminates your soul, bringing life, vitality, and joy.

So if vocation means "calling," then it makes sense that calling comes in the form of an inner voice that speaks into our soul in a deep way. To hear that voice, our souls must become still enough to listen. Author Parker Palmer speaks of the soul this way: "Like a wild animal, the soul is tough, resilient, resourceful, savvy, and self-sufficient: it knows how to survive in hard places. . . . Yet despite its toughness, the soul is also shy. Just like a wild animal, it seeks safety in the dense underbrush, especially when other people are around."[5] When I think of the quotes about modern womanhood, I think about the first half of this quote—the savvy, tough, independent part of our souls. But when I think about our calling, I think about the second half of this quote—the wild and untamed part of us that is also shy and hard to find.

I think it requires courage to seek out this part of your soul because it's easy to fear you'll never find it. Perhaps you fear that if you get still enough and wait long enough, you'll come up empty. Or perhaps you believe, as I once did, that calling is reserved for the ones who are *really* going to make a difference in the world. Perhaps you have decided you must not be important enough or gifted enough or good enough to pursue an adventurous, purposeful life. Maybe you've avoided silence and the questions because it's taking way too long for God to get in touch with you. Maybe you believe you missed his call, and since he's God, he doesn't have time for you anyway.

My friend, if I'm describing you, would you allow me to try to speak truth to this shy, fearful part of your soul? If I could scoot close to this part of you and wait for it to venture out of the thick covering you've made out of sufficiency and self-protection, here's what I would whisper:

God has a deep affection for who he's made you to be.
He has counted you worthy of a calling.
Living your calling takes courage.

If you are brave enough to proceed, here are some truths to listen for and grab hold of to find that beautiful intersection of God's light and your life:

You are gifted.

As a mom, one of my least favorite words is *gifted*. That's because many parents in my community go into a gifted frenzy about the time their kids enter third grade. Teachers introduce a parade of tests and assessments. Children are evaluated, and the academically advanced are identified. "Portfolios" are created. My poor kid still can't tie his shoe, and yet a portfolio of his skills already exists, tucked in a file folder somewhere with his name on it.

In the classroom, *gifted* is the word used to describe a certain kind of kid who can do certain kinds of things (which usually involve #2 pencils and Scantron sheets). *Gifted* is reserved for the special few. *Gifted* means you have potential and you'd better live up to it. If you aren't gifted, what are you? Regular? Remedial? Almost gifted? Not close to gifted?

Because we have such strong academic associations with the word *gifted*, it can be hard to interpret this same word as applied in Scripture. No wonder we may assume that some people are gifted and some are not. Maybe you don't feel like a *gifted* Christian—just a regular one, or a remedial one, or a not-quite-gifted one.

But the Bible describes giftedness in an altogether different way. It isn't reserved for a certain tier of intelligence or talent. It's not measured using the kinds of tools we use on one another. It's measured only in the limits of God's supply—so in other words, no measurement can contain it. It has no limitations, and it defies all assessments.

The Greek word for gift is *charisma*. In our culture, we use the word *charisma* to describe that special talent that sets someone apart—and we use it particularly to describe those who have some form of celebrity. It's a word for those on the red carpet, or those who lead companies or teams to victory. But charisma is a solid Jesus word, so let's reclaim it! In the Greek language, the word has *charis* at the center—meaning grace. The suffix *-ma* means "the results of." So charisma is about grace and the results of that grace. Charisma is the power that comes when God's light hits our prism of a heart and bursts into glorious color. And because grace is our unmerited, unearned, undeserved gift of salvation, not reserved for any special group, then charisma—"the results of grace"—is for everyone. Every single one of us who says, "Jesus, I need you" is given the instantaneous, all-sufficient *charisma* for our particular life—in both general ways (grace) and specific ways (gifts). In Christ, we are all gifted. *You are gifted.*

And what's more, this verse combines that charisma with "call." As Paul said, "God's gifts and his call are irrevocable" (Romans 11:29). The *call* is the invitation from God to live it out. It's as if God is saying to you, "There are three things I need you to know: I've gifted you, I've invited you, and no one can take back that gift or invitation." It's the ultimate no-refund policy on this incredible, powerful offer of living in grace and manifesting the result of that grace. We are *all* gifted.

I haven't included a list of these gifts in this book. You can find some of the manifestations of spiritual gifts listed in 1 Corinthians 12, 1 Corinthians 14, and 1 Peter 4. But throughout the Bible, you'll find that God calls people to wild jobs, and not all of them are listed in those passages. God called Noah to build a massive boat when there was no rain. God called Gideon to be a mighty warrior when he had no army. God called Esther to protect her people when she had no authority to make those decisions. God called Peter to be his rock even when Peter was a loose cannon. God called Paul to be his chosen mouthpiece when he was in the middle of persecuting Christians. God will keep calling people until the work in the world is done. And you don't have to spend much time in the world to know that the work is not done. So whether you find a very specific gift in the passages listed here or whether God uses you in another creative way to build up his people around the world, you are, without a doubt, called and gifted—and those two are related.

Your gifts point to your calling.

Your gifting becomes the foundational element to understanding your calling. You may find that discovering your specific gifts feels complicated. But remember that God has a deep affection for you and a passionate love for his creation. He wants you in action, in sync with the way he's wired you. In fact, Scripture has a great deal to say about our gifts:

God wants you to know and use your gifts. First Corinthians 12:1 says, "About spiritual gifts, brothers and sisters, I do not want you to be uninformed." God is not trying to hold back and make it hard for you to figure it out. But he does require you to pray in faith, bravely and boldly, and to promise him to use this power, this *charisma,* for whatever needs to get done to point the world back to him. Remember: "A spiritual gift is given to each of us so we can help each other" (1 Corinthians 12:7, NLT).

We are all gifted, but we are not all gifted in the same way. First Corinthians 12:4 tells us, "There are different kinds of gifts, but the same Spirit distributes them." We are made for specific and different purposes, but for the same goal—to build up the Kingdom of God. Not sure how to discover the way you're gifted? We'll explore that further on pages 151–155.

The purposes of the Kingdom—the call we all share—trump the specific gift, our individual call. We are called first to advance his Kingdom, and secondarily we are called to a specific way of using our gifts. Let me share a story that might help clarify the way our charisma works together.

I was working part-time in student ministry at Hope Church,

helping lead Sunday evening youth group. Our youth group looks like most typical high schools, and I'm proud of that. We have a mix of sporty, spicy, preppy, and "angsty" teens. We attract kids who've been raised with Jesus and those who have never heard his name. It's a very unchurchy atmosphere that attracts some very unchurchy kids.

One particular Sunday night started off no differently from any other. The students streamed in the front door in all their dyed-hair, ball-cap-backward, short-skirt, selfie-taking glory. Our volunteer youth staff was busy working on their normal roles—preparing food, welcoming kids at the door, gathering last-minute supplies for a messy game, strumming their guitars, or looking over their teaching notes. In that crew of volunteers, some were leaders; some were administrators. Some were great behind the scenes and some were great with the kids in the corner. In a normal scenario, all of us work in our gifts, weaving together our different skills for one united purpose.

Just as we were about to begin our program, a friend and coworker of mine approached me. He told me that a fifteen-passenger van had just run off the road on the highway near our church. A group of teenagers from a Mennonite church, traveling home from a mission trip, was on the side of the highway while the leaders of the trip were medevaced to two different hospitals in Richmond. One was assumed dead. The state trooper called to the scene knew about our church and wanted to know if we could provide shelter for the shell-shocked teenagers.

Here's the thing: We don't have a plan B for sheltering Mennonite teenagers whose leaders are in critical condition. But this wasn't the time to worry about who was gifted for what.

We all laid down our jobs and our "gifts" and did what was right in this new plan. We sprang into action. I went to the hospital with the kids who were related to the leaders, to sit with them and provide guidance while they navigated a technologically advanced world very different from their own. Another volunteer gathered belongings from the wrecked van, while other students repurposed our snack (pizza) and made a quiet space for our guests to gather and rest.

In another room, my friend sat our teens down on the floor and began to lead them in prayer. It was an incredible sight: our students, who looked like they'd just come from a teenage reality show; and the other students, who looked like they had just walked off the set of *Little House on the Prairie*. But in this moment, that didn't matter. Our students didn't even seem to notice as they went to work serving, cleaning, praying, and responding to what God had placed in front of them.

Several hours later, we had found housing, clothes, and food for the Mennonite teenagers who would stay in town with their injured parents. We provided hospitality, leadership, intercession, and administration. Because although we were all created with specific gifts, that night demanded that we lay down our preferred roles to do whatever needed to get done.

That might seem like an extreme example, but it does illustrate an important point when it comes to our calling. We were all created for a specific purpose, but sometimes our gifts need to take a backseat to what needs to be done immediately. Likewise, when it comes to the call of God, it isn't about any one person getting glory or always working only within her gifts. It's about God getting glory for the work he's called us to do. It's about being a team. So we bring specific gifts but always for a common purpose. That night with the Mennonite youth group, we all had one goal in mind: to serve our brothers and sisters in their time of need. Most of the time, our volunteers work within their gifts at youth group, and at other times, we do whatever is necessary to get the job done and bring God glory.

Now let's apply this to our lives. We all have a common purpose and work to do, which we will talk about in a moment. In general, we will do our best work and find it most enjoyable when we are using our specific gifts. But there will be times in our lives when it's all hands on deck. There might be whole seasons of life when our gifting and circumstances just don't line up. But sisters, if you are in a season like this—raising toddlers when you want to work, working when you want to raise toddlers, feeling stuck in a church that doesn't seem to work for you, following when you want to lead, administrating when you want to create—wherever you find yourself in this season, you can trust that it won't be like this forever.

> *Sometimes God uses seasons of mundane, anonymous service to uproot pride and insecurity and sow in his charisma.*

Sometimes the things that are hard for us instruct us about who we are really made to be. Sometimes the seasons of mundane, anonymous service are times when God digs deep into the soil of our hearts, uprooting the unworthy roots of pride and insecurity and deeply sowing in his charisma—the results of his grace.

God gifts us for his glory, not our own. Our charisma enables us to love what God loves, so that together we are "like living stones . . . being built into a spiritual house" (1 Peter 2:5). We become the visible and outward expression of God's invisible nature. This creates a clear filter for us when we are exploring our calling. We can ask ourselves, *Am I most concerned with being able to do or be this person for God's glory or for my glory?* I've often heard my pastor and friend, David Dwight, say it like this:

> Most of us see ourselves as the main character in the story of what we want our life to be. Everyone else in our life becomes the supporting cast that's supposed to fall into line with the vision we have for our lives. But God is the main character, and he doesn't do glory competitions with us.[6]

Perhaps when you are ruthlessly honest with yourself, you resonate with this. Maybe you can think about how you want life to play out, and the role you want everyone else to play to make it work. If you've ever thought, *If they would just do x* or *If only I had x,* then maybe you know what I'm talking about. And it can be tempting to think about the way we want to use our strengths for our glory rather than for God's.

But to lean into charisma is to promise God, "I want what you want." This is a simple expression of our desire to surrender our lives to him and to live under his lordship. It means no matter what comes—whether good or bad, painful or joyful—we can continue to say to God, "Your will be done."

In Jesus, we find the one we are to imitate. We see Jesus expressing love and relationship to everyone, particularly the "less loved" of society. We see Jesus expressing God's justice by treating each and every person—kids, women, the despised, the ill, the homeless, the beggars—with this tender and powerful love that upholds them as treasured in the eyes of God. He teaches us to give our charisma freely to all those around us, in order that we might shine God's light into the world.

God isn't restricted by our self-imposed limits. Most of us don't need more gifts; we need more courage to believe in the gifts we already have! We need to have faith that God can use us despite what we consider our limitations and weaknesses. We've all been given an important to-do list, and it's not limited by our season or circumstances in life.

We've all been given an important to-do list, and it's not limited by our season or circumstances in life.

We put limits on ourselves, fueled by self-doubt, all the time. You might think, *If only I had this education* or *If only I had these experiences* or *If only I had a mentor.* We see mountains where God sees speed bumps. We see oceans where God sees puddles. But if he's calling you to climb that mountain or cross that ocean, he will sustain you for the task. That mountain may be a relationship you don't think will ever change. That mountain may be your anxiety about your own worth. Your ocean may be the school debt that you don't know how you'll ever pay off. Your ocean may be facing a life that seems empty or lonely.

Not only does God know exactly where you are right now, he knows where he's taking you. He has the benefit of seeing the whole story played out—the past, present, and future. He actually has the plan, and whatever you are dealing with is part of that plan. He has not forgotten you; in fact, he's chosen you to work his plans to completion. He's made you his masterpiece (Ephesians 2:10, NLT). You are part of his plan A for bringing his love to the world, for working his plan of rescue, for restoring dignity and worth to all human beings.

So you don't have time to worry about the mountains or the oceans. You just need to get going. You just have to start climbing and then let him "make level paths" (Hebrews 12:13) over that mountain. You wade into the water and trust that he'll pile up the waters to make a path through them (see Exodus 15) if he's calling you across the ocean. God will make a way forward; your work is to believe him.

The Bible says that "the eyes of the LORD range throughout the earth to strengthen those whose hearts are fully committed to him" (2 Chronicles 16:9). When you give God your fully committed heart and say, "No matter what, no matter who, I want to express your love for the world," you should expect miracles to happen.

The supernatural presence of God may become evident in the conversation with your coworker or in the way you sing a worship song. It may express itself in the love you feel for someone from your church who's cranky or insecure or needy. It may be seen in the way you devote time and money to fight injustice or in the way you serve a friend by watching her toddler for the night. It may show up in the way you are present and listen to those around you. These are the miracles of God moving passionately in you when you give him your whole heart. This is the charisma. This is the gift.

And when every single one of us expresses our charisma to the full, we come together in this beautiful symphony. Our lives become music. Each of us plays a part in this symphony, music expressed into this world that says, "Hallelujah! Salvation and glory and power belong to our God" (Revelation 19:1).

Brave Enough to Explore Our Gifts

I've found that women have a hard time pinpointing their gifts without someone else confirming what they see in them. Often, learning about our gifts happens best in our community of friendships—in our book club or small group or with a trusted friend or mentor. Together, we can gently and hesitantly tell the stories of what we've always wanted to be—of the dreams we've had, or the ways that we think we may have heard God speaking to us. We can talk about the holy moments when we suspect that God has been present. We can encourage and affirm and challenge one another to embrace who God made us to be and to find our calling.

At its most basic level, using our specific gifting

- brings us joy,
- benefits the world, and
- taps into the deepest part of our souls.

One of my friends describes how she feels when she's expressing her calling like this: "Even when I feel exhausted at the end of a day of serving, somehow I also feel so satisfied and refreshed in it." When you are expressing your gifts, you feel a sense that God has dipped deeply into the coldest, purest, most refreshing part of his heart and poured that out in you. You feel refreshed and renewed. You might find that your soul is quieted in the midst of your service, as you are in awe of who God is. You might cry or laugh or feel energized, like something is happening both outside of you and inside of you.

These moments are sacred because they are when you are completely in step with the Holy Spirit, bringing him great joy and receiving great joy in return. It might take years of struggle and confusion to find the courage to believe in your gifts, to find the place to express your gifts. But it is so good and so satisfying that when you get there, even the toughest journey feels worth the work.

The Four Facets of Calling

Parker Palmer says, "Before I can tell my life what I want to do with it, I must listen to my life telling me who I am."[7] I believe that the use of our gifts, the confirmation of our gifts, timing, and God's voice all point us toward our calling. Our calling becomes the thing we cannot *not* do. The following figure, along with its related questions, might help you as you listen to your life telling you who you are. These are not necessarily questions you can answer immediately. You might find there's much you aren't sure of or don't know. But that's okay! Remember that exploring your calling takes courage, but also time, experience, and the willingness to venture out of yourself and try different things.

I hope you'll find this figure helpful in discerning the four facets of your calling. Exploring who you are allows you to be more sensitive to what God is calling you to do (or not do). When your eyes are open to your abilities, you are more likely to respond to a need when you see it and to know that you are the one to address it! But don't get too rigid by trying to force everything to line up. God is going to call and equip you with gifts that will build up his church—and he will draw on an infinite variety of skills and experiences.

I love the creative people I work with. They are incredibly talented graphic designers, photographers, and technicians.

They use their gifts to build up the church. They are all gifted as servants, attending to the background work that removes distractions and allows people to worship. In our culture, in this day and time, God has gifted them with an incredible ability to harness technology to build up the church. The

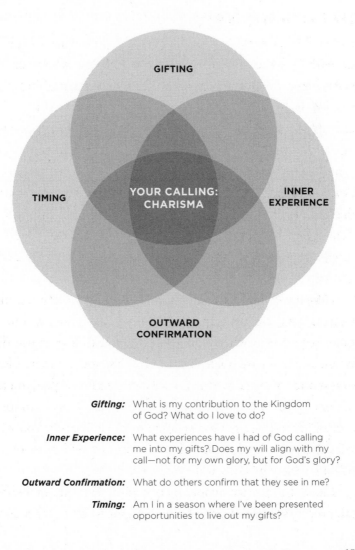

Gifting: What is my contribution to the Kingdom of God? What do I love to do?

Inner Experience: What experiences have I had of God calling me into my gifts? Does my will align with my call—not for my own glory, but for God's glory?

Outward Confirmation: What do others confirm that they see in me?

Timing: Am I in a season where I've been presented opportunities to live out my gifts?

outworking of that gift—the way it fits into this world—isn't listed in the Bible. But it's a modern means to an ancient end. It delights God because it builds up his church.

If you have the gift of teaching, God may work through you as you volunteer in your child's classroom, as you encourage a friend over coffee, as you facilitate a small group for your church, or as you speak to thousands from a stage. If you have a gift of mercy, God may work that out as you leave a note for a coworker, as you buy a meal for a homeless man, or as you help fund a major initiative in Ethiopia.

The gift you've been given will not be contained to one season of life. You'll find that it is a common thread through your life, even from your early years. When your soul is allowed to speak, you'll find that it keeps saying the same thing. Even if you feel frustrated and *certain* that there's no way God is going to align your passion for serving with an opportunity to serve, take heart! God loves doing the impossible when you trust him with his timing, his purposes, and his plan.

Brave-enough women don't have to know exactly what God's made them to do, but they are willing to find out. Together, we can all take a step forward in this. We can quiet our souls to listen and pray for one another so that we will have the strength to be still. We can gently hold up one another's dreams and listen carefully and fully as those around us gingerly share these precious and vulnerable parts of their hearts. And when we see a prism in another that breaks into a glorious rainbow, we can tell her, "I see you. I see who you are made to be!"

Brave-Enough Pause

Parker Palmer says, "People take copious notes on what retreat leaders say, or what certain wise people in a group say, but rarely, if ever, do they take notes on what they themselves say."[8]

In exploring our territory, we must let our lives speak to us. We must quiet down enough to let our souls come out from the underbrush of the hurried and loud patterns of our days and actually tell us about who we are truly made to be.

Our Daily Brave

Take ten minutes with only a journal and pen. Write a one-sentence life mission statement. It may start with "I exist to . . ." or "My life mission statement is to . . ." A couple of rules: You can start with something general, but it should also contain something specific. You may want to say, "I exist to serve God," but try to finish the sentence "I exist to serve God through . . ."

This is meant to be a little scary and hard. But try it. See what comes forth. Scribble and scratch out and erase but put some words on paper. This is a beginning.

Come back to your sentence this week. Read it again, and share it with a friend or your small group. Ask others if it rings true for you.

Pray

We began this chapter with the question, "Who am I?" So now I ask you to pray bravely and boldly with me:

Heavenly Father, will you give me the courage to believe that you've given me gifts? I ask you to help me look fearlessly into my own life and heart and believe you. Give me the boldness to say yes to this great strength you've gifted me with.

CHAPTER 8

Brave-Enough Women Know Their Limits

I am glad to boast about my weaknesses, so that
the power of Christ can work through me.

2 CORINTHIANS 12:9, NLT

IT HAPPENS MORE OFTEN than I want to admit.

Once again, I had overscheduled myself. Because my work is ministry, almost every meeting happens in the evenings or on weekends—and I was running late, again, as I prepared for another one this Sunday afternoon. There was the preparation—making copies and picking up lunch for everyone. In the midst of scurrying around, racing the clock, my thoughts turned to yet another meeting I had to lead over dinner and the several e-mails I had to take care of in between. I was also mentally composing a grocery list and trying to figure out when I'd fit in a trip to the store so that the kids would have lunch before the school week started. I knew I also needed to schedule the carpool for the upcoming week—for three different practice and game schedules. And did I mention the birthday party I was hosting in between my two meetings that day?

As my lunch meeting dragged on, I began to worry. At 1:48 p.m. I panicked and quickly ended the meeting. *I had given myself a twelve-minute margin to get to my own child's birthday party.* By now you may be feeling a little (or a lot) anxious on my behalf because clearly I had not learned anything about leading, mothering, or throwing birthday parties if I thought I could do all these things in one day.

I raced to the party, pulled quickly into a parking spot, ran inside, and grabbed my daughter from my husband, who had sprung to the rescue (again) to help me make it all work. A few minutes later, I stood next to one of my closest friends, who asked me what I was up to. When I casually mentioned that I was writing this chapter on limits, she began to laugh at me. Hysterically laugh. Like, not even a "trying to be polite about laughing" laugh.

"Are you serious?" she snorted at me.

I tried to keep a straight face and feign innocence. "What? Why are you laughing at me?"—at which point, I also burst into hysterical laughter, because, Hello. I should not be writing a chapter on limits.

Unless, of course, we are all in this together and none of us is perfect. Unless life isn't about doing it right, but about being brave enough to keep growing. Because let's be real: I'm terrible at limits. I blow by my own boundaries so fast I can't even read the speed limit sign. I pile on the commitments and plans and say yes willy-nilly with almost no regard for balance, boundaries, or health. So feel free to laugh with me.

What makes us act like we are unstoppable, unflappable,

unlimited? Is this kind of frantic lifestyle, this hectic inner pace what God designed us for? And if not, why is it that it takes so much resolve to say no, to embrace our limits, to face the truth that we may disappoint or even frustrate people around us with our choices?

I wonder if we could be brave enough together to be ourselves and nothing more.

I wonder if we could be brave enough together to be ourselves and nothing more. To actually make choices—to say yes and to say no—and to do it with peace. If that sounds like an attractive but unattainable goal, I'd love for you to join me as together we try to understand how to take what God's given—our boundaries—and live within them.

Limits and Calling

You might wonder why this chapter on limits comes right after the one in which we explored calling. You might think this is the wet blanket on top of the little flame you've just felt ignite in your soul. But exploring calling and limits together makes sense. Sometimes it takes a great deal of courage to say no to good things in order to have the courage to say yes to the right things. Knowing my own struggle with setting limits, I reached out to friends online to find out whether they struggle with them too. My friend Mila quickly responded, saying, "When I'm living without boundaries, I don't know how to say no to myself."

Even good gifts become a curse when we operate outside of the boundaries God places on our lives. Even our God-given calling becomes an idol when we charge forward without Christ as our Lord—the one who is actually leading our lives. Mila goes on to say that outside her boundaries, she feels "unstoppable—not in a mighty and strong way but in a possessed-woman-on-a-mission kind of way." *Possessed-woman-on-a-mission?* Sounds just like my recent Sunday! Perhaps you can also relate to days like the one I've described—when you frantically move from one activity to the next, trying to juggle it all and do it all with grace.

My friend Stacie says that once she's blown past her limits, her days feel like a "craziness snowball where I can't stop/won't stop." A life without limits—*even when pursuing good things*—ignores the boundaries God has placed on our life. When we ignore our limits, we strive forward as if we were not finite, limited creatures. In some ways, we act immortal—as if our own bodies, minds, and souls don't have a capacity to them. But the price we pay for this relentless pace is high. Peace is fleeting. The ability to hear God's voice wanes. When we are beyond our limits, we do not "keep in step with the Spirit [of God],"[1] the only one who is actually without beginning, end, or limit. Our heavenly Father has a design for our lives, and it does not involve striving, being anxious, or reactively accepting obligations that have gotten out of control.

So yes, living within our limits takes courage. It also requires us to take stock of what really matters so we can set those appropriate limits. Then we must take steps to bring our calling into line with our boundaries as we pursue a life that's free of this craziness.

Why is it worth working on? Because a woman who knows that she is limited and that boundaries are good is a woman at peace. And a woman at peace is wonderfully attractive. I have a friend like this. When I am with her, I feel as if I'm the most important person in the world. She isn't distracted or rushed. She seems particularly attentive to the vibe around her—yet somehow she's like a neutralizing agent for stress.

She allows others to embrace their own limitations and be okay with them.

This is a woman who's faced many limitations in her life. Maybe that's why she's a woman who really prays, like all day long. She's a woman who is very thoughtful about her choices and isn't afraid to gently but firmly say no when she's outside of her limits. Sound impossible? Maybe . . . but doesn't it sound wonderful? Doesn't it sound like something worth working toward?

A woman who sets limits for herself allows others to embrace their limitations and be okay with them.

So if you want to go ahead and admit that "no" feels like a bad word in your vocabulary—if you want to confess that you worry, maybe even a lot, about what will happen if you slow down—then maybe you have difficulty setting limits too. Maybe you can admit that you are living at an exhausted, joyless pace and that you know that something isn't right in your soul when your schedule is out of control. Let's admit that we can struggle at setting limits and still seek God together in it.

Why We Hate Limits

There are no witnesses to corroborate her story, but my mom *alleges* that, as a little girl, I used to stick a body part over the threshold of the door of my bedroom whenever I was "grounded" to my room. I cannot confirm or deny this story, although I do seem to remember waking up from a tantrum-exhausted nap with rug marks on my cheek. Apparently, I've always had an uncomfortable relationship with limits.

What is in us that tempts us to put our toes over the line? What makes a toddler scream "no"? What makes us push the limits—whether by trying to sleep less, stay up later, eat a little more, or meet everyone's needs? There seems to be a driving force within us that wants to stretch, to expand, even, perhaps, to live forever. Though we are *wired* for eternity and immortality, we can't get around the fact that we are housed temporarily in a finite, decaying shell—our body.

You might think that my jumping from a story about a childhood tantrum to suggesting we often live as if we're trying to defy death is a big leap, but denying our limits is a cultural obsession.

- We try to break limits all the time. *Guinness World Records* alone catalogs over 40,000 different kinds of records.
- We buy up anti-aging everything—to an estimated price tag of 249.3 *billion* dollars in 2012. That's in *one year.* And researchers project that we will spend 345.8 billion dollars on these products and services by 2018.[2]
- We look for ways to circumvent our need for sleep. Starbucks uses 2.3 billion paper cups per year. Their biggest cup, the Trenta, holds more coffee than your stomach's entire capacity.[3] We are overfilling and outcaffeining our own organs.
- We race against the clock. We get more efficient. We multitask. We say, "Yes, we can" even when our bodies and our souls are groaning, "No, we can't." As my friend Tiffany says, "I know I can, so I do."

Everyone who responded to my question about limits admitted that she was living outside her boundaries. We do it. We regret it. And we do it again. There seems to be a battle within us—one part of us pulls hard for peace and surrender; the other part pushes hard to rebel, to work beyond our capacity—to do more, be more, have more, live more.

Perhaps we are wired with this tension for a reason. Perhaps God has given us two great gifts—great capacity and great fragility. Perhaps it is when we acknowledge the beauty of enabling the two to function together that we discover a deep truth about ourselves and about our God. We are, indeed, "treasures in jars of clay" (see 2 Corinthians 4:7), and yet God has something to reveal about his all-surpassing power as he works through these ever-limited bodies of ours.

Jesus and Boundaries

Jesus is the greatest expression of how we are to live in the reality of both power and limitations. Hebrews 4:15 says, "We do not have a high priest who is unable to empathize with our weaknesses." Jesus, our high priest—the one who is able to make amends for our sin and restore our relationship with our Father—this Jesus knows what it's like to be limited, to be human. Jesus was tired (John 4:6); Jesus was hungry (Mark 11:12); Jesus was thirsty (John 19:28). Jesus mourned and wept (John 11:35). He was deeply distressed (Mark 14:33). Jesus felt abandoned and forsaken by his own Father (Matthew 27:46). He was misunderstood by his earthly mother and brothers (Mark 3:2, 33-35; John 7:5).

Jesus felt deeply the limitations of humanity and experienced with agonizing precision the humiliation, torture, and pain that humans can inflict on one another. Jesus gets it. Certainly Jesus came to earth to astonish us through the mystery of the Cross, which makes us right with God. Yet Jesus also sent a strong message simply by living with a finite, limited body just like ours. Jesus came as a man and showed us how to live in light of the Father's great power and in great humility within the limits of our own frail bodies.

Following Jesus' example by surrendering and accepting these limits can be the key that unlocks the grandest places of intimacy and relationship with Christ that we will ever know. The journey into our weakness is a trip toward a tangible, can-almost-touch-it experience with the presence of our great God. This tangible experience isn't something we can drum up for ourselves. For me, it has come mostly through hardship and challenge.

Repeatedly in my life, God has brought me to a place of the surrendered prayer of "enough." My enough prayer is the place of exhaustion where I cannot go on without him—where I'm too tired or too worried or too controlling and I know my methods just aren't working. The enough prayer is a declaration of surrender.

> *Enough, God. I can't do this anymore.*
> *Enough, God. My plans stink.*
> *Enough, God. I keep messing up when I'm working*
>   *without you.*
> *Enough, God. I'm so tired of worrying.*
> *Enough, God. Please come to my rescue.*

It's in this place of weakness—and only in this place of weakness—that I've found myself willing to truly give God all of my heart, all of my plans, all of my desires. I want to believe that I'll grow to truly give myself to God without having to come to *enough*. But I'm also so grateful that it's in this place of weakness where Jesus says that his power is made perfect, where he can be more than enough.

This is not a journey for the faint of heart. Facing our limits—our own "enough"—often means facing our greatest fears. Embracing our weakness, our smallness, and our frailty in life is terrifying. We have to admit that we cannot do it all. We have to admit that we might not be all we thought we could be, that the people around us might not like us, that we might feel things we'd rather avoid—like boredom, loneliness, anger, or despair. But at the core, living within boundaries—recognizing even the difficult pain in life—means we recognize our humanity. Reaching our limits means we recognize our need. And from this place of humility we find grace. Oh friends, it's always about *grace*. And God's Word has much to teach us about the paradox of glorious freedom that comes when we admit to those limits and choose to live within boundaries.

Boundaries and the Bible

So what is a boundary? On a basic level, a boundary is a limit set on your life. A boundary is like a fence around your personal property. There are limits that are true for everyone—like our body's need for water. But there are also personal limits—unique to each of us and our wiring. Boundaries are the measures put in place to respect our limits.

Who sets the boundaries? The Bible makes it clear that God is the one who knows healthy boundaries for our lives, and his commands are about "choosing life" (see Deuteronomy 30:19) in the way we live and love. Because God also gives us freedom, some of those boundaries are easy to breach—either willfully or accidentally. Boundaries might feel like picket fences—easy to jump and ignore. Other times, God makes those boundaries more like fifteen-foot-high brick walls. As much as we smack into them, God won't let them move.

Our relationship with God's boundaries is explored in Psalm 16:

You are my Lord; apart from you I have no good thing. (verse 2)

Life Rule #1: We need the continual reminder that God has created a way for us, and living under his authority in an everyday commitment to Christ is where we find we will be the fullest expression of ourselves. Living apart from him doesn't lead to anything good.

You have assigned me my portion and my cup. (verse 5)

Life Rule #2: God sets the portions and he fills the cups. He determines what we (truly) need, and he provides for those needs.

The boundary lines have fallen for me in pleasant places; surely I have a delightful inheritance. (verse 6)

Life Rule #3: God creates the boundaries, and then he calls them good. God is not surprised by anything in your life. He uses boundaries for your growth and protection, and he calls them good.

The life you are living—described as your portion, your cup, your boundaries—is God's design, and he calls it good.

Think about that for a minute. The opportunities you have and the ones that haven't happened. The relationships you have and the ones you wish you had. The way your body reacts to sunlight, bedtime, exercise, and food. All of it is in God's design. All of it.

Go ahead, protest. I do. Go ahead, think of the "buts . . ." you have for God. Think of the circumstances that you can most assuredly promise God are *not good*. Think of the opportunities you deserve and the relationships that need to be righted. Think of the dreams you have and the desires you want to see fulfilled. Bring the whole lot before him and give it all over.

Say to the Lord, "This is what I want my boundaries to be." If you're like me, you might want to stand in front of him and put your hands on your hips and yell them out. You might be tempted to throw an inner tantrum and tell him *how it should be.*

But then. Then hear him say to you:

> "Should you not fear me?" declares the LORD. "Should you not tremble in my presence? I made the sand a boundary for the sea, an everlasting barrier it cannot cross. The waves may roll, but they cannot prevail; they may roar, but they cannot cross it."
>
> JEREMIAH 5:22

You see, God's love for you is not weak—it's fierce. God's design for your life isn't haphazard—it's chosen. God's boundaries for you aren't an accident. Despite the shoreline's ragged edges, no storm can cross the line that God puts into place.

This portion he's given you—these boundary lines he calls pleasant—they are *for you.* God's design for the ocean limits its reach. God's design for the night limits its reign. God's design for the sun means it rises and also sets. He sets boundaries over all of his creation—including us. His boundaries mean we cannot be all, do all, or even serve all. Nor are those boundaries the same for everyone. He shapes us individually, uniquely, painstakingly into the exact vessels he needs so that his grace will reach "more and more people" (2 Corinthians 4:15). We do not lose heart—we do not lose our courage—because we know that God uses the boundaries he has specifically placed around our lives to shape and mold us for his use.

God, in his great love for us, invites us to live as the people we are, not the people we want to be. He invites us to know both the power of the treasure we hold within us as the dwelling place of Christ and the fragility of the jar of clay in which the treasure rests. He invites us to run free within our boundaries while honoring our limits.

Our Limits

The first step to embracing our limits is knowing what they are. Our limits come in a variety of forms:

Physical limits: Our need for sleep, good food, exercise, and reflection.

Time limits: Our bandwidth; our ability to manage and use time well.

Emotional limits: Our ability to express ourselves; our willingness to be vulnerable; our need to understand and recognize how emotions drive our actions.

Season-of-life limits: Our changing demands throughout life. The needs of our families, friends, and careers deeply impact our own choices and ability to act on our calling.

Individual limits: Our unique capacities. We are intricately and uniquely wired, which means that one person's capacity will be different from another's. We may all be jars of clay, but the jars are different sizes.

Spiritual limits: Our guidelines from God's Word; his sovereign work in our lives, which may limit us for reasons we cannot explain; God's choices for the way we should live, which, when we follow them, are known as "obedience."

Boundaries help us know our limits and stay within them. Our boundaries are driven by the priorities we determine for our lives. For instance, if I value soul health, I will place boundaries around things that exceed my soul's limits. This could be a decision like: *Because my soul doesn't thrive when I am filled with unrealistic expectations of love, I will place a boundary around the kind of music I listen to.*

The Red Lights of the Soul

We may recognize and agree that we all have boundaries and they are worth staying within, but sometimes we recognize them only when we've already breached them. How do you know when that's happened? I think at the heart, living outside our limits leads to an absence of both peace and joy.

When we exceed or fight against any of our limits—physical, emotional, spiritual—for an extended period of time, we notice a conspicuous lack of peace. Our souls feel wound up, whirring like an engine on high. We have a sense that we just can't turn off the engine. Even those activities that usually work as temporary respites—like a good workout, an hour to ourselves, or a girls' night out—won't do the trick. We've exceeded our limits so far beyond what's reasonable that we don't know how to reestablish boundaries.

Maybe you can relate to some of the ways women have told me that they know when they've overstepped their limits:

"I have anxiety attacks. All I want to do is get up and flee to my home to cry, be frustrated, and then nap from pure exhaustion." –Kate

"I pushed God away for a long time and decided to make all my own choices for my life. Looking back, I actually felt burdened living outside my limits, though everything I was doing was supposed to be 'fun,' which really shouldn't bring burdens at all." –Megan

"I start 'leaking out.' Someone kindly said to me, 'How's the business going?' and I blurted out a laundry list of anxieties—I just couldn't hold them in. Later I imagined him thinking, *Wow, I just kind of meant in general*... He got a lot more than he bargained for!" –Linda

"Outside my limits, I find I can't enjoy where I am but am always pressing on to the next thing." –Brittany

"When I live outside my limits, I shut down. It's like I become paralyzed, and I stop talking to people and go into my shell. My pride gets the best of me, and I'm ashamed that I can't handle it all." –Joanne

"The minute I start feeling like I'm showing up everywhere but I'm never present—that's when I've exceeded my limits." –Rachel

There are limits that are obvious from the outside (stage of life, need for sleep, etc.), but many limits involve our inner life. And we cannot compare our inner lives to those of other people. Stacie says it this way: "Living within my limits means living within *my* limits, not anyone else's." We are just too complicated, with too many buttons and levers, to expect that one size will fit all when it comes to limits.

Some of us may be able to get up early, go for a run, make breakfast for our kids, send off some e-mails, and kiss our husbands as they leave the house—all before 7 a.m. Others of us may be deeply focused on and attentive to just one area of life, finding that multitasking and full calendars actually make us *less* of ourselves, not more. We are, in fact, not "every woman." Each of us is only one woman, one individual person with physical, emotional, and relational limits. We can never be both the fullest expression of ourselves and at the same time be everything to everyone. And the more we try to be everything, the less we are able to actually be ourselves.

> We can never be both the fullest expression of ourselves and at the same time be everything to everyone.

One weekend I sat in the bleachers at my son's baseball game. It was a beautiful day; the sun was still warm but the hint of fall was in the air; the sky was a deep blue punctuated by puffy white clouds; the air smelled of freshly cut grass. The excited *whoop-whoop*s of little boys filled the air as they shimmied around the infield, kicking up dust and punching their mitts, eager to start the action. The day could not have been more beautiful. And I barely noticed it.

I had been going hard—driving forward with a new school year, a new babysitter, a new project at work. The whole family was going through one transition after another—new schools, new teachers, and new schedules. I needed to go directly to work from the game, and as the minutes ticked by, I grew increasingly restless. When the coaches decided to keep the game going for a few extra minutes, I found myself irritated. I didn't have those ten minutes to spare—at least I didn't feel like I did. I fidgeted on the bleachers and checked my e-mail on my phone (again).

Just then, one of the boys ran up from the dugout and planted himself in front of his mom. "Is Dad coming?" he asked. She sighed and breathed out heavily. "I don't know." The little guy ducked his head when she answered and then walked slowly back to the dugout.

All these observations collided at once—my irritation at sitting there for an extra ten minutes, the little boy wishing for his dad, the beautiful day—and I thought to myself, *Things are not right.* It is not right when I'm pushing my own limits so hard that I cannot sit outside and enjoy it. It is not right when I lose the joy of simply being the parent who shows up at the baseball game, knowing that it means so much to our kids. It is not right when ten extra minutes of joy for my son make me feel like my whole day is going to fall off track. You see, it is not the circumstances we must look to when it comes to our limits—it is the fruit of those circumstances. If the fruit that my life is bearing looks anything like my attitude at the baseball game, I need to prune the tree because that stuff is *ugly.*

Because I wasn't willing to acknowledge my own need to slow down; because I wasn't brave enough to let an e-mail slip by, to disappoint someone, to cancel a meeting, I had been pretending I could do it all. Meanwhile, my own soul was feeling strained, joyless, and anxious, and I was not able to be my full and free self for anyone.

Trying to be everyone makes me not good for anyone.

We each experience emotions, process relationships, and order our lives differently. Our demands are different, our capacities are different, and our support structures are different. But if we are willing to do a courageous self-examination, if we are willing to let the fruit of our lives teach us about what's at the core of our being, then we are able to know our limits, obey our limits, and grow from our mistakes. Here are some questions you might ask yourself during your self-evaluation:

- *Regardless of the demands on my time, are my closest relationships thriving?* How your husband, kids, and/ or closest friends feel about your limits says a lot about whether you are living in them.
- *In the midst of it all, do I feel a deep stillness in my soul?* When Christ is at the center of your activity, you will find a deep, unshakable place of rest within you.
- *How am I doing at saying no?* Are you saying yes out of fear of disappointing someone or letting someone (including yourself) down? Do you struggle with a fear of missing out or being passed over? When's the last time

you said no so that you could say yes to something (or someone) more important in your life?

- *Am I making time for the regular boundaries (good food, regular sleep, exercise) needed to maintain my physical health?* There will always be seasons when you feel stretched, but have you neglected your body's needs for a prolonged time?
- *When I do find moments of rest, am I able to actually rest?* A brave-enough woman knows how to work and how to rest. If you find that you are unable to downshift from "go" mode, you may have exceeded your limits.
- *Am I finding joy, wonder, and whimsy in my days?* Nothing shows more trust in God's plan than the ability to laugh during the day, find wonder in the small things, and celebrate the silly and whimsical in the world.

That afternoon on the baseball field was a perfect picture of what life looks like for me when I'm exceeding my boundaries. You see, God promises us a full and abundant life with him. He calls us to use our specific gifts to bring him glory and to build up one another. But what he always calls us to first, middle, and last is *love*. And usually when we exceed our limits, we begin to lose that. We lose our affection for the people we are closest to. We lose our love for ourselves, neglecting and abusing our own bodies. We lose our love for the world, feeling irritated rather than compassionate toward those around us who seem to expect so much of us. (I actually felt that the Starbucks lady was too demanding the other day when she was clarifying my drink order. Hello, I'm a walking nightmare. Busted-limit alert!)

Because God always, always places love at the center of our

obedience to him, when we are having problems loving, we have *big problems*. When we lose our ability to love, we need to put the brakes on fast and ask God to redirect our steps. If we can't find joy in the busyness, find peace in the storms, find love for people—then we need to find our way back to the path God has marked out for us. He is a sustainer and a provider, and we will always find peace when we live in obedience to him.

> When we lose our ability to love, we need to put the brakes on fast and ask God to redirect our steps.

We can find *soul rest* in the middle of complete chaos when we are close to Christ. We can find *soul revival* even in the most tiring, demanding seasons of life when we are leaning into Christ. We can find *soul redirection* in the ways we've gotten off course when we are kneeling before Christ. For the hard things he's given us to do, he can provide strength and peace. For the hard things we've brought on ourselves, we can find forgiveness and courage to change. We truly find everything we need for a full life *lived within our boundaries* when we seek God's will for our lives.

So before we go further, let me tell you one thing about limits: Limits are not about *balance*, like the kind talked about on magazine covers. It's not about how long you spend reading your Bible or having a quiet time. It's not about taking a nap. (Okay, sometimes it might be about taking a nap, but it's not *just* about that.) We aren't talking about a prescription for how you should live your life. Remember that for each of us, life is different, and so our demands are different.

God may be calling you to endure one of the hardest seasons a woman could ever go through. You may laugh at the idea of limits because you are so bone-crushingly tired from being a single mom, or a college student working two jobs, or a mom of teenagers who's also caring for a declining parent. You may be up to your eyeballs in demands that you can't get out of. So what I don't want you to hear is a prescription for how to live your life, or more rules for you to follow. That's not how Jesus did it, and he was always vehemently opposed to those who did. He hated when religious people added the wrong kind of burdens to people's lives. And so when we talk about living in our limits, this isn't about shaming you into some rigid existence. It's about discovering true *rest* for your soul.

Sabbath: Old School

The concept of rest is introduced early in the Bible, in the Creation account in Genesis. After God created everything, the Bible says, "The heavens and the earth were completed in all their vast array" (Genesis 2:1). God then created a space and time for rest: "By the seventh day God had finished the work he had been doing; so on the seventh day he rested from all his work. Then God blessed the seventh day and made it holy, because on it he rested from all the work of creating that he had done" (verses 2-3). It's an interesting twist to the story. God, who is infinite and perfect and who has no need for rest—God, who is the owner and operator of time—chose to create another day and designate that day for rest.

There's a sense as you read the account that the rest completes the Creation—that without this day to pause, the Creation itself would not be complete. It reminds me of sitting down before a beautiful table on Thanksgiving. Rather than just diving into the food, everyone usually pauses to admire and cherish the work that went into creating this beautiful event. In designing the Sabbath, God created this part of our work—the part where we remember what's been done and enjoy the results of it. He modeled resting on the Sabbath for us as well—not because he needed it, as if God could be tired.

As the story of God's people progresses throughout the Old Testament, the emphasis on Sabbath remains. Keeping the Sabbath is one of the Ten Commandments given to Moses by God: "Remember the Sabbath day by keeping it holy. . . . The seventh day is a sabbath *to* the LORD your God" (Exodus 20:8, 10, emphasis added). The word "to" is interesting. It tells us that the Sabbath isn't *for* God. It's an act of obedience *to* God. One commentary says, "The Sabbath was a covenant sign of God's authority."[4] When we rest from our work, we acknowledge *to* God his ultimate authority over us. We acknowledge that he is the source of our life and energy, and he is the keeper of our days. We acknowledge that he is "my Lord; apart from you I have no good thing" (Psalm 16:2). We pause on the week and express gratitude for the gifts—large and small—that God has given each one of us. From our eternal life with him to the food on the table, Sabbath invites us to remember and rejoice in the multitude of gifts we receive from God's hands.

So when we honor our limits, we acknowledge God's authority. It's about *obedience* to our heavenly dad. It's as simple as following his house rules.

Sabbath: New School

In the New Testament, Jesus often tussled with the Pharisees over the Sabbath. You see, God's people had started adding to the rules. It was true that Sabbath was a big deal. Resting from work and acknowledging God's authority was important to

God and important for his people. Sabbath created a space that set the Israelites apart. It created a rhythm for the community, a time to worship, to hear God's Word, and to remember together their communal story—that God was the rescuer who had freed them from bondage. The Sabbath reminded the Israelites that their freedom wasn't designed to allow them to run around willy-nilly, doing whatever they wanted, but that their freedom had a purpose. One Jewish rabbi, speaking of the freedom celebrated through Passover celebrations, said it this way,

> We were liberated from Egypt not to wander as free spirits in the wilderness but for a purpose—to serve God. The words are interesting here—we escape from "avodah kasha" ("difficult labor"), which the Egyptians forced upon us, to "avodat Hashem" ("worship of God") and a system of life that God reveals.[5]

Sabbath became part of that *system of life*.

But in calling out the religious leaders for adding to the rules and making them burdensome, Jesus revealed our human propensity to take the essence—the spirit behind them—of God's rules and turn them sideways. We *all* do this. We do it when we chase fake grace. We do it because we want to be able to figure out life without God. We create a system of rules and hoops that make life safe and certain rather than wild and unpredictable. We want to think, *If I just do A, B, and C; God will love me and will bless me with D, E, and F.* We make up rules and make things hard so we can prove to ourselves we deserve his blessing.

This was the Pharisees' attitude. Whenever Jesus did something that didn't fit into their religious system—teaching, healing, conversing with the "have-nots"—they got fired up. They threw around scriptural knowledge and got furious at Jesus when he didn't follow their prescriptions. And they loved to do this with the Sabbath. They got mad at Jesus when his disciples ate grain from a field on the Sabbath. They got mad at him for healing people on the Sabbath. They lost sight of the big rule—love—because they were chasing their little rules. Jesus clarified his position with those old-school rules when he said, "The Sabbath was made for man, not man for the Sabbath. So the Son of Man is Lord even of the Sabbath" (Mark 2:27-28).

Jesus didn't remove the spirit of the Sabbath (rest and acknowledgment of God's authority), but he placed himself *over* the Sabbath. He is the Lord of that rest. He is the governor of our soul-restoring Sabbath. We don't find it in rigid formulas or in a certain amount of sleep or in how much time we spend in church on Sundays. We find it in our Lord, the Lord over soul rest. When we are close to Jesus, when we are obedient to our heavenly Father's house rules, when we submit ourselves to that authority, we find true rest. We find peace with our limits and courage to be just who God has made us to be—no more and no less.

It takes courage to agree that God is right on this one— that our bodies and souls need a break. To be brave enough to embrace our limits is to accept our flawed, worn selves as precious and in need of care. It means there are times when we leave the house messy so we can snuggle with our toddlers. It means there are times when we say no to a volunteer opportunity so we can sneak in that walk with a friend. It means there are times we don't color-code our calendar so we can preserve our staring-out-the-window time.

It means we intentionally carve out space for nothing, *and we don't beat ourselves up over it.* It means we choose life-giving ways to spend our time, combating our own propensity to over-schedule or distract or numb ourselves to Sabbath rest.

The Gift of Limits

So rather than seeing our limits as . . . well, limiting, Jesus invites us into the experience of Sabbath rest. Sabbath rest is an expression of quietness, of stillness, of relaxation. Rather than a law of Sabbath, which worked from the outside in (follow this law and actually rest from everything for a full day), Sabbath rest is a rule of life that works from the inside out (be still in your soul and experience the fruit of that in your whole life). The concept of this inner rest comes from Hebrews 4:9-11, which says,

> There remains, then, a Sabbath-rest for the people of God; for anyone who enters God's rest also rests from their works, just as God did from his. Let us, therefore, make every effort to enter that rest.

Sabbath literally means "to cease." We will accept our limits only when we realize how good this inner Sabbath rest actually is for us. And we will know how good it is only when we actually begin to embrace it. What does this kind of Sabbath rest do for us?

1. Sabbath rest for our souls allows us to cease striving.
2. Sabbath rest for our souls allows us to hear God.
3. Sabbath rest for our souls restores our desire for God's desires.

It takes courage to pursue this kind of rest. Sometimes it reveals hard things. As one friend said, "I think I'm worried that if I slow down, I'll discover some feeling I don't want to deal with or some truth I don't want to be reminded of." We allow frenetic activity in our lives and in our souls to serve as a cover. We keep ourselves busy in order to feel worthy. We keep ourselves busy to distract ourselves from pain. We keep ourselves busy so we don't have to deal with our own struggles. But in doing so, we deny our own limits. We bully our own souls.

Because it takes courage to know our limits and enter into Sabbath rest, the writer of Hebrews doesn't tell us to "embrace" Sabbath rest or to "fall into" Sabbath rest or even to "choose" Sabbath rest. He says, "*Make every effort* to enter that rest" (emphasis added). We have to make the effort. We have to work for it. We have to fight off the demons of busyness, distraction, and doubt. We have to pry apart the doors to the deepest rooms of our heart, and go there and rest. We wait. We wait for God to do what only he can do. No matter how hard we try, we cannot do God's work for him. We cannot give our souls rest, revival, or redirection. Only God can.

Making this effort means pursuing moments of quietness when you actively place yourself in God's presence. You might think that you are in a season where that's not possible, but I imagine that each one of us could find ten quiet minutes in a day. Sometimes the quiet comes when you are doing routine chores, like dishes or laundry. It might come when you turn off the radio and choose silence on your way to work. Quietness can come in a quick walk around the block, or in the moments right after the baby goes to bed. This place of quietness where we actively place ourselves in God's presence has a fancier name: contemplative prayer.

Author Ian Cron says that this kind of silence with God is transformative. "It's not in the moment [that I feel changed] . . . but seven hours later, I find myself in a situation where I'm more patient with someone who I am typically impatient with. . . . It was this morning when I silently gave God consent to whatever he wanted to do in my heart and my soul."[6] It's in those silent places of consent that God has a place to speak to us—to beckon us to rest, to trust, to be still, to believe. Sabbath rest can't be defined by one moment or one set of rules. It is an inside-out setting of our soul where we enter into God's presence, the most restorative, relaxing, renewing place we can ever experience.

Sabbath rest is an inside-out setting of our soul where we enter into God's presence.

Here is what God promises when we rest in his presence and authority:

The eyes of the LORD range throughout the earth to strengthen those whose hearts are fully committed to him.

2 CHRONICLES 16:9

You will seek me and find me when you seek me with all your heart.

JEREMIAH 29:13

If any of you lacks wisdom, you should ask God, who gives generously to all without finding fault, and it will be given to you.

JAMES 1:5

You do not have because you do not ask God.

JAMES 4:2

When we make the effort to enter God's rest, we can uncover the greatest riches of his promises. We find wisdom—we know when to say yes and when to say no. We find courage—not only to listen to his commands but to do them. We find peace—because in that deep soul-center runs the living water of Christ, where we will never be thirsty again.

"Come to me, all you who are weary and burdened, and I will give you rest" (Matthew 11:28). This is the promise of our Savior, the Lord of the Sabbath, and the pathway to Sabbath rest. It is in his presence that we find the courage to live in our limits. A Hasidic proverb says, "We need a coat with two pockets. In one pocket there is dust, and in the other pocket there is gold. We need a coat with two pockets to remind us who we are."[7] The gold feels like the real gift—but the dust is just as important. It's with an understanding of our calling and our limits that we experience an ever-deepening trust in the path God has for us and the ability to enjoy that path, even when we don't know where it's going.

Our calling is our great strength. Our limits are our great weakness. And in the intersection of our calling and our limits is that deep place of rest—the place where we discover when to say yes and when to say no. It's the place where God tells us when to wait and when to go. It's where we receive coaching and correction and confidence. It is our secret weapon in a world gone mad for multitasking and frenetic activity.

Another recent Sunday started much like the one I described at the beginning of this chapter. People and obligations; rushing from one appointment to the other. But I had a quiet moment as I stood over the sink, loading the dishwasher that morning. In that moment, I took a deep breath and settled my heart

LEARNING LIMITS

Do you struggle to accept limits and make choices? If so, here are some techniques that might help:

Ponder: **Know who you want to be.**

Imagine a week of your life that feels healthy and balanced. What do you envision? Are you making dinners? Working out? Spending time for God? Now choose the top three things that feel important to you. Write them down somewhere prominent so they are in front of you. It's important not to choose too many at once—that would overwhelm you.

Prioritize: **Know your yeses and nos.**

Now that you have a sense of what's most important to you, you can create a yes/no meter. The next time you face a scheduling decision, use this default sentence: "When I say yes to _____, I am saying no to _____."

For instance, during a busy season of writing for this book, I had to choose between early morning workouts or quiet time to write. I said to myself: *I feel called to write this book as a priority for this season. In order to say yes to writing, I've said no to running with a friend for the next three weeks.* Prioritizing your yeses makes you more aware of the choices you are making and reminds you of your limits. It places the responsibility for your schedule back where it belongs—on you. It empowers you to also say no to something when you realize the impact it would have on your priorities.

Prepare: Create a default statement.

In order to stick to your priorities, you need an escape method for decisions that want to break through your boundaries. Have a sentence at the ready that allows you to default a decision. When asked to take on a new responsibility, don't say yes right away. Instead say something like, "I'll have to check my schedule and get back to you." This allows you time to think before you act.

Practice: Form the letters n-o.

If you struggle with your no, start small. The next time a salesperson asks you to consider buying more, simply say, "No, thank you." Don't make an excuse or give the person any room to continue the conversation. That will make it easier to say no the next time an acquaintance or even a friend asks you to do something that would exceed your limits. Again, politely say no. Don't make excuses, tell a story, or make it emotional. All of those answers sound like "no, but maybe" instead of "no, not ever." Once you've practiced in small ways, step it up and try it with a bigger decision.

in God's presence. Sometimes I do this by imagining I'm in front of the throne of grace, there to receive what God has for me that day (see Hebrews 4:16). Sometimes when I do this I'm reminded of a verse or passage in Scripture (the result of years of practicing the spiritual survival skill of Word!). On this day, words from Proverbs 3:5 settled into my mind: "Trust in the LORD with all your heart and lean not on your own understanding."

I then felt a quiet sense from God: *You don't have to figure everything out. You can trust me.*

I held a plate midair, literally coming to a complete stop. I asked myself, *Is that from God?* Immediately several other Scriptures quickly came to mind:

"The LORD will fight for you; you need only to be still" (Exodus 14:14).

"Some trust in chariots and some in horses, but we trust in the name of the LORD our God" (Psalm 20:6).

"'Not by might nor by power, but by my Spirit,' says the LORD Almighty" (Zechariah 4:6).

Because I have come to know God's Word, I was quickly able to confirm that those words that had quietly appeared in my heart were trustworthy and true. God really doesn't need me to figure everything out. I can trust him.

I smiled over the sink. God loves me. He knows me. He speaks into my life with tenderness and grace. I can trust him.

The day was still busy, the to-do list was still long, but I was different. I said no to an event that I wanted to attend but that didn't really fit into my schedule. It was hard to do it, but I felt brave enough that day.

I'm not embracing my limits perfectly, but I'm learning as I go. And I'm realizing that God truly wants to teach me to rest in his grace and authority. God wants to change me, and he often does it in deep, almost imperceptible ways. My job is just to make every effort to get still in his presence.

I have never experienced more pain in my soul than in facing my limits. But I think it might be the kind of pain that's more surgical than wounding. I think it's the kind of pain that leads to more freedom, not less. Limits are a harsh but needed teacher. Limits remind me to look in the mirror every morning and declare, "I am not God." Limits tell me that I am finite but I have an infinite heavenly Father. Limits shape me into a vessel God can use.

Brave-Enough Pause

Our Daily Brave

Reflect on the following verse:

> He said to me, "My grace is sufficient for you, for my power
> is made perfect in weakness." Therefore I will boast all the
> more gladly about my weaknesses, so that Christ's power
> may rest on me.
> **2 Corinthians 12:9**

Now read it again but insert your name and your weaknesses
into the verse:

> He said to me, "My grace is sufficient for you, _____
> _____ [your name], for my power is made perfect
> in _____ [your specific weaknesses]."

Therefore I will boast all the more gladly about my weak-nesses, so that Christ's power may rest on me.

2 Corinthians 12:9

What would it look like to "boast about your weaknesses" this week?

Pray

Father, you've made me a mighty treasure in a fragile vessel. Help me to embrace both the power and the fragility of my life, placing myself under your authority. God, today I claim that "apart from you I have no good thing," and I claim that my boundary lines are pleasant and good. Meet me with your presence and peace as I submit myself to your limits.

CHAPTER 9

Our Daily Brave

People have no idea what one saint can do: for
sanctity is stronger than the whole of hell.

THOMAS MERTON

No one wants to get a knock on her hotel room door in
the middle of the night. And when that knock is an insistent
pounding; and when you aren't expecting it; and when it's just
you, a friend, and your two young daughters sharing a suite—
that knock is terrifying.

The first knock came at 3:12 a.m. I heard it, vaguely, and
quickly pulled myself out of bed. After tiptoeing toward the
door, I peered out of my window. Nothing.

Walking slowly back to the bed, I glanced around our room,
which looked a bit worn and weary even in the dim light coming from outside. I'd found this hotel on the Internet when my
friend and I were planning a trip to our daughters' gymnastics
meet. The rooms didn't look quite as grand as the pictures

online made them appear—and the hotel's website hadn't mentioned that the doors opened to the outdoors.

Just as I finally began to drift back asleep, someone pounded on our door again. My eyes flew open and landed on the large red numbers on the clock: 3:40. I hurried toward the door and looked out the peephole. This time I saw a man standing right outside. I was scared—the kind of scared you feel in every cell of your body.

A million thoughts ran through my head. My logical side knew that this guy had probably just gotten lost on the way to his own room. My illogical side began running through every other possibility, none of which were good. I yelled something through the door to him, and he responded.

I couldn't make out what he said . . . but he did walk away.

I sat on the couch in our little hotel living room and reached for the phone. I called the front desk. No answer. I called housekeeping. No answer. I called the main hotel line. No answer. I started dialing again—front desk, housekeeping, outside line. Still no answer.

As I sat there waiting, my hands shaking in my lap, I considered the irony that I'd just made some of my final edits to this book earlier in the day and here I sat, nearly *freaking out*. After I tried the front desk several more times, someone finally picked up. A security guard came to our building to check on things. The man never came back. I am almost certain he was just lost. But in the stillness between 3:40 and 3:50 a.m., I felt anything but brave.

Yet I'm not so sure that is true. As my friend Kristy says, "You can be scared and strong." And in that quiet, scary hotel room, I'd forced myself to remember some truth: Being brave enough in that moment was about realizing that I wasn't alone. That God's love is always with me, even when I'm scared and can't necessarily feel it. Of course, it doesn't take pounding on a hotel room door to scare us. Scary takes all kinds of forms, from forgiveness to saying no to having truthful conversations.

We started this book together with the question, "What makes us brave?" Answering that question took us on a journey into our inner world—the place where we experience the love of Christ and its impact on the rest of our lives. When we are truly loved, we can feel secure in the midst of scary circumstances. We feel safe to be the fullest expression of ourselves. We feel free to be wrong, knowing we will still be okay. We feel strong enough to face difficulties and fears. We are healed when we know that we are loved.

We talked at the beginning of the book about how much we need Jesus-courage. We need the kind of courage that comes from Jesus' presence in our life, from Jesus' work in our life. Both his presence and his work flow out of God's magnificent love for us. It is his love that brings good. It is his love that brings change.

The Outworking of Love

As I sat, heart pounding, in that hotel room, I realized I could do nothing to fix the situation or to eliminate all the danger. Being brave enough simply meant waiting on God—and giving all of myself to him. When we give him all we have, that's more than enough for him to work with. And he works with us, all right. He exposes us to true grace and teaches us to let go of any "different Jesus" we may be following. He calls us to repentance and forgiveness for ourselves and for those who have wronged us. He calls us to truth in our words and in our actions. He teaches us about our specific calling, and he teaches us to live in our limits. And through it all, we are becoming brave. We are becoming less fearful and anxious and more peaceful and still. We are changing—sometimes in ways that we could scarcely imagine.

Being brave enough simply means waiting on God—and giving all of yourself to him.

One of the young women on my team at church walked into my office the other day. Because I have been studying how God's love changes us, I dropped a question on her. "Chelsea, do you think of yourself as a saint?" (Even in our church office, this was a rather strange question for me to ask.)

Chelsea laughed and shook her head no.

So I turned to my other coworker and said, "Paige, do you think of yourself as holy?" She laughed harder.

We don't use words like *saint* and *holy* to describe our lives. Maybe we think those words are too good and too pure for us. Maybe we think that those are old words for a former time and that they aren't relevant or cool or modern. Maybe we assume we can't possibly put together a bold and beautiful life with words like that.

But the Bible tells us something different. The Bible tells us that knowing God changes us at the deepest level. When we really allow God to reveal himself to us, we experience the equivalent of a molecular change in our spirits. When we know this incredible love of God, when we receive his great love for us, we enter his presence, and in that presence something . . . well, *holy* happens.

This is our God; this is his greatness! He has no equal and

he is comparable to no one. There is no one like him in heaven or on earth because everything he's made is a mere shadow of him. But everything beautiful in this world—the clouds painted across a blue sky, the smell of a baby's skin, the taste of a ripe strawberry, the soft, fresh furriness of a tomato leaf— every beautiful thing is just a small reflection of his beauty, his creativity, and his majesty.

Isaiah 40 is a poetic character study of our God. It says that he "brings out the starry host one by one and calls forth each of them by name" (verse 26). He's a majestic and meticulous God—he both created the stars and knows each one of them. He can call every star that you see scattered across the sky by name—and every one that you cannot see! That same verse assures us that "not one of them is missing." Imagine that—our God is so big and yet so attentive that not even one star in this mighty universe can disappear without him noticing.

Yet not only does he have universal vision, he also has personal vision. Isaiah 40:11 tells us that God is also close and always present, leading us tenderly, like a shepherd with his lambs. So this same God who hung the stars and set the moon in place also carries his lambs—us—close to his heart.

The more we bask in this powerful and personal love God has for us, the more we are changed. It's really that simple. The more we know that our powerful and personal God is interested in us, delighted in us, mighty to save us, shepherding us, leading us, loving us—well, the more we change. The power of God's love is best expressed in the word we keep talking about—grace. It is his steadfast and undeserved kindness for us—in our weakness, in our failures, even in our sinfulness—that leads us to repentance. Repentance is the way we turn—turn away from our own path and onto his. We talked in the last chapter about getting on Jesus' path and living within his boundaries—and that's the way we turn. Jesus says in Matthew 3:8 that we should

The more we bask in this powerful and personal love God has for us, the more we are changed.

"produce fruit in keeping with repentance." When we follow Jesus on the path he has set out for us, we are walking on a fruitful path, one that leads to the fullest and freest life we can experience.

So what makes us brave? Love makes us brave. And it does more than that. God's love also makes us holy.

Love makes us holy

Holiness can be a weird word that conjures up some strange images in us. Things like nuns, maybe. Or monks. Probably something that seems old and boring. But let's reclaim that word for what it's really about.

At the core of it, holiness refers to the transformation God sparks within you when he dwells in you. Ephesians 4:24 says that we "put on the new self, created to be like God in true righteousness and holiness." Nothing is holy in its own right—God chooses to make someone holy: "Something holy is that which has been brought into relationship with God . . . and designated by God as having a sacred purpose or special significance to him."[1] Because God calls us his "masterpiece" (Ephesians 2:10, NLT), because he decided that our new, restored selves are "created to be like God," we are made holy. It has absolutely nothing to do with our pedigree or our history.

God decided whom he would set apart to call holy. He decided to do that with you—scared, feeble, and fickle as you may be! You are his chosen and special possession, and he has decided that you are plan A for expressing his glory and love in the world. You and I may not understand why this seems like the best plan, but he knows what he is doing. So he calls us holy—and that's not all. He calls us *saints*.

And now we are saints

As if holiness wasn't enough, we have a new identity in Christ— as *saints*. Psalm 85:8 says that God promises "peace to His people and to His saints" (NKJV). The Hebrew word for saint— *hasiyd*—comes from the same root as *hesed*, which is a significant word in the Old Testament that describes God's grace. So if a working definition of *hesed* is grace, then a *hasiyd*—which we translate as saint—would literally be a "person of the grace."

We've been made a holy people because God decided to set us apart for this significant purpose. We may have a hard time thinking of ourselves as saints, but what if we considered ourselves "a people of the grace"? What if we were characterized not by a self-righteous, condescending religiosity but instead were known as people who radiate grace? That's a definition I can get behind because that's the kind of woman I want to be. That's a label we can proudly wear.

God's great power, great strength, and tender and passionate love for people are at the core of our new, transformed selves.

> We are "a people of the grace."

There's a sense of settled, at-rest belonging in our souls when we find our place with God. There's a sense of letting-go surrender when we allow him his full and rightful reign in our hearts. His love shines out of us because we are allowing it to shine within us. This is holiness. It is the outworking of God's grace. We may not think of ourselves as mighty warrior princesses. We may not feel like we can take on the world. But we can be brave enough for today, knowing that it is commitment to God that makes us holy—that gives us access to this "new self."

Author Elisabeth Elliot says it this way: "The fact that I am a woman does not make me a different kind of Christian, but the fact that I am a Christian makes me a different kind of woman."[2] This is the journey of holiness. It is a beautiful and simple story of surrender, of trust, and of an unshakable hold on the faithful promises of God—both now and into eternity.

Pursuing this holy life drives away fear. Pursuing this life frees us to be "holy through and through."[3] And oh sisters, what God can do with hearts fully devoted to him! What God will do when we give him the very best of ourselves—when we abandon our wills to his way and when our full and honest hearts say, "Not my will, but yours be done." This is the wellspring of our courage. This is what makes us brave.

Brave Enough

So this has been a story about courage—what makes us strong. But it's mostly a story about grace. It's about how love changes us. It's about this incredible adventure that God has invited us to be in together. It starts and ends with courage. We take Jesus seriously with courage. Then we train ourselves for spiritual strength. We learn to receive grace and give it. We face the fights. We explore our territory. We embrace our limits. We take up our daily cross and live our daily brave. This is what it means to be a saint of God. This is what it means to grow in holiness. We are a people of the grace. We are the women set apart. We are strong and we are brave because we serve a mighty

God, our provider, our protector, our strength, and our shield. So take heart, women, take heart.

We aren't training for earth; we are training for heaven. There will come a day when God will come for us. It may be the end of our earthly lives or it may be when Jesus returns to earth to "judge the living and the dead" (2 Timothy 4:1). But the time is coming for all of us. We are women with a mission. We've been given a job to do—to take our ordinary selves and allow God to transform us into bold, beautiful, brave women with hearts that go after what his heart goes after—a passionate love for his people and a desire for all to "be saved and to come to a knowledge of the truth" (1 Timothy 2:4).

So as we end this chapter together and close this book, I would like to spur you onward with the words of the prophet Isaiah, designed to "encourage the exhausted, and strengthen the feeble" (Isaiah 35:3, NASB). The Lord gives us courage with this truth about what is and what is to come:

A highway will be there;
    it will be called the Way of Holiness;
    it will be for those who walk on that Way.
The unclean will not journey on it;
    wicked fools will not go about on it.
No lion will be there,
    nor any ravenous beast;
    they will not be found there.
But only the redeemed will walk there,
    and those the LORD has rescued will return.
They will enter Zion with singing;
    everlasting joy will crown their heads.

> Gladness and joy will overtake them,
> and sorrow and sighing will flee away.
>
> ISAIAH 35:8-10

No more sorrow. No more sighing. No more fear—only gladness and everlasting joy. This is what is before us, women of the grace.

So we are righteous. We are free. We bravely follow God wherever he leads. The word *amen* means "it's true." So together, let all of us, every brave-enough woman reading these words, say, *Amen.* It's true.

Brave-Enough Pause

Our Daily Brave

As you worked through this book, what one or two key takeaways did you discover?

Based on your own study of Scripture or review of the "Word on Courage" appendix that begins on page 199, what phrase or Scripture passage best captures how you are growing in Christ in this season? What has God been teaching you about yourself and about him?

Finish this sentence: Because God makes me brave enough, I can _____. Make it as specific as you can for whatever you are facing right now. You might want to record it in your journal as a marker of your relationship with God in this season.

Pray

Father in heaven, I come before your throne of grace with confidence. I am brave enough because you provide for me in my weaknesses, you strengthen me for your work, and you love me with an everlasting love. I want to live that as my deepest truth in every day that you give me, until I meet you face-to-face. Amen.

The Word on Courage

BRAVE ENOUGH is about the courage we discover through a relationship with Jesus Christ. This courage is a result of grace—God's lovingkindness—a force that changes us from the inside out. No matter what life throws at us, the confidence we find in God's grace enables us to move forward—taking one brave-enough step at a time.

Because God extended his grace to us "while we were still sinners" (Romans 5:8), it's never a result of work we do outside of ourselves. In surrendering to his grace, we can be honest about our weaknesses, even as we cling to the external power that makes us brave.

You may have noticed Scripture woven into the chapters of this book. When it comes to reading the Bible, I've heard it said that the Bible is not like a group of Post-it notes on a fridge, full of disparate pieces of advice. Nor is it like an encyclopedia, designed to be a "look up" resource for any number of needs. The Bible is altogether different. It is the Word of God, "alive and powerful. It is sharper than the sharpest two-edged sword, cutting between soul and spirit, between joint and marrow. It exposes our innermost thoughts and desires" (Hebrews 4:12, NLT).

Scripture helps us to see ourselves as we really are, but God also uses it to effect real change in our lives. As you seek to be more courageous in the months and years ahead, I encourage you to plug into this power source. For easier access, I've collected many of the passages from this book and arranged them by theme: God's passion for us; his power and protection; his priorities; his promises; and his provision. As you seek his counsel on one of those topics, I pray you will find a word that encourages and strengthens you.

Before you dive into these Scriptures, may I offer a few suggestions? Don't just read a passage or verse; think about it as you go about your day. Don't just write a Scripture down in your journal; write it on your heart by memorizing it. God promises that we will seek him and find him when we seek him with our whole hearts (see Jeremiah 29:13). Devote your heart to knowing him, and he promises he will reveal himself to you. What a promise!

God's Passion for Us

The LORD God formed the man from the dust of the ground. He breathed the breath of life into the man's nostrils, and the man became a living person.

GENESIS 2:7, NLT

I say to the LORD, "You are my Lord;
    apart from you I have no good thing." . . .
LORD, you alone are my portion and my cup;
    you make my lot secure.
The boundary lines have fallen for me in pleasant places.

PSALM 16:2, 5-6

He tends his flock like a shepherd:
 He gathers the lambs in his arms
and carries them close to his heart;
 he gently leads those that have young.

ISAIAH 40:11

He turned around and said to them, "If you want to be my follower you must love me more than your own father and mother, wife and children, brothers and sisters—yes, more than your own life. Otherwise, you cannot be my disciple. And you cannot be my disciple if you do not carry your own cross and follow me. But don't begin until you count the cost."

LUKE 14:25-28, NLT

Out of his fullness we have all received grace in place of grace already given.

JOHN 1:16

Greater love has no one than this: to lay down one's life for one's friends.

JOHN 15:13

In him we live and move and have our being.

ACTS 17:28

I commit you to God and to the word of his grace, which can build you up and give you an inheritance among all those who are sanctified.

ACTS 20:32

If God is for us, who can be against us?

ROMANS 8:31

By the grace of God I am what I am, and his grace to me was not without effect.

1 CORINTHIANS 15:10

We have this treasure in jars of clay to show that this all-surpassing power is from God and not from us.

2 CORINTHIANS 4:7

The grace that is reaching more and more people may cause thanksgiving to overflow to the glory of God.

2 CORINTHIANS 4:15

God made him who had no sin to be sin for us.

2 CORINTHIANS 5:21

God saved you by his grace when you believed. And you can't take credit for this; it is a gift from God. Salvation is not a reward for the good things we have done, so none of us can boast about it. For we are God's masterpiece. He has created us anew in Christ Jesus, so we can do the good things he planned for us long ago.

EPHESIANS 2:8-10, NLT

God our Savior . . . wants all people to be saved and to come to a knowledge of the truth.

1 TIMOTHY 2:3-4

But you are a chosen people, a royal priesthood, a holy nation, God's special possession, that you may declare the praises of him who called you out of darkness into his wonderful light.

1 PETER 2:9

Look, I am coming soon!

REVELATION 22:7

God's Power and Protection

The Lord will fight for you; you need only to be still.

EXODUS 14:14

The joy of the Lord is your strength.

NEHEMIAH 8:10

Some trust in chariots and some in horses,
   but we trust in the name of the Lord our God.

PSALM 20:7

Wait for the Lord,
   be strong and take heart
   and wait for the Lord.

PSALM 27:14

Encourage the exhausted, and strengthen the feeble.
Say to those with anxious heart,
"Take courage, fear not.
Behold, your God will come with vengeance;
The recompense of God will come,
But He will save you."

ISAIAH 35:3-4, NASB

He made my mouth like a sharpened sword,
   in the shadow of his hand he hid me;
he made me into a polished arrow
   and concealed me in his quiver.

ISAIAH 49:2

Today I have made you a fortified city. . . . They will fight against you but will not overcome you, for I am with you and will rescue you.

JEREMIAH 1:18-19

"Should you not fear me?" declares
     the LORD.
  "Should you not tremble in my
      presence?
I made the sand a boundary for the sea,
   an everlasting barrier it cannot cross.
The waves may roll, but they cannot
     prevail;
   they may roar, but they cannot cross it."

JEREMIAH 5:22

Jesus immediately said to them: "Take courage! It is I. Don't be afraid."

MATTHEW 14:27

The words I have spoken to you—they are full of the Spirit and life.

JOHN 6:63

Sin shall no longer be your master, because you are not under the law, but under grace.

ROMANS 6:14

The Spirit helps us in our weakness. We do not know what we ought to pray for, but the Spirit himself intercedes for us through wordless groans.

ROMANS 8:26

May the God of hope fill you with all joy and peace as you trust in him, so that you may overflow with hope by the power of the Holy Spirit.

ROMANS 15:13

So now I am glad to boast about my weaknesses, so that the power of Christ can work through me.

2 CORINTHIANS 12:9, NLT

I pray that out of his glorious riches he may strengthen you with power through his Spirit in your inner being, so that Christ may dwell in your hearts through faith. And I pray that you, being rooted and established in love, may have power, together with all the Lord's holy people, to grasp how wide and long and high and deep is the love of Christ.

EPHESIANS 3:16-18

We know, brothers and sisters loved by God, that he has chosen you, because our gospel came to you not simply with words but also with power, with the Holy Spirit and deep conviction.

1 THESSALONIANS 1:4-5

Let us then approach God's throne of grace with confidence, so that we may receive mercy and find grace to help us in our time of need.

HEBREWS 4:16

Hallelujah! Salvation and glory and power belong to our God.

REVELATION 19:1

God's Priorities

> Write these commandments that I've given you today
> on your hearts. Get them inside of you and then get
> them inside your children.

DEUTERONOMY 6:6-7, MSG

> Man does not live on bread alone but on every word
> that comes from the mouth of the LORD.

DEUTERONOMY 8:3

> Test me, LORD, and try me,
>   examine my heart and my mind.

PSALM 26:2

> Teach me your way, LORD,
>   that I may rely on your faithfulness;
> give me an undivided heart,
>   that I may fear your name.

PSALM 86:11

> God blesses those who work for peace, for they will be
> called the children of God.

MATTHEW 5:9, NLT

> Love your enemies! Pray for those who persecute you!

MATTHEW 5:44, NLT

> If you forgive anyone's sins, their sins are forgiven; if
> you do not forgive them, they are not forgiven.

JOHN 20:23

> I consider my life worth nothing to me; my only aim is
> to finish the race and complete the task the Lord Jesus

has given me—the task of testifying to the good news
of God's grace.

ACTS 20:24

I urge you, brothers and sisters, in view of God's mercy,
to offer your bodies as a living sacrifice, holy and
pleasing to God—this is your true and proper worship.
Do not conform to the pattern of this world, but be
transformed by the renewing of your mind. Then you
will be able to test and approve what God's will is—his
good, pleasing and perfect will.

ROMANS 12:1-2

Make every effort to do what leads to peace and to
mutual edification.

ROMANS 14:19

Since we live by the Spirit, let us keep in step with the
Spirit.

GALATIANS 5:25

Don't grieve God. Don't break his heart. His Holy
Spirit, moving and breathing in you, is the most
intimate part of your life, making you fit for himself.
Don't take such a gift for granted. Make a clean break
with all cutting, backbiting, profane talk. Be gentle
with one another, sensitive. Forgive one another as
quickly and thoroughly as God in Christ forgave you.

EPHESIANS 4:30-32, MSG

Set your minds on things above, not on earthly things.

COLOSSIANS 3:2

We labor and strive, because we have put our hope in the living God, who is the Savior of all people, and especially of those who believe.

1 TIMOTHY 4:10

Let us throw off everything that hinders and the sin that so easily entangles. And let us run with perseverance the race marked out for us.

HEBREWS 12:1

Let us continually offer to God a sacrifice of praise.

HEBREWS 13:15

Be alert and of sober mind. Your enemy the devil prowls around like a roaring lion looking for someone to devour. Resist him, standing firm in the faith.

1 PETER 5:8-9

We love because he first loved us.

1 JOHN 4:19

God's Promises

The eyes of the LORD range throughout the earth to strengthen those whose hearts are fully committed to him.

2 CHRONICLES 16:9

I will hear what God the LORD will speak,
for He will speak peace
to His people and to His saints;
but let them not turn back to folly.

PSALM 85:8, NKJV

Trust in the LORD with all your heart
    and lean not on your own understanding;
in all your ways submit to him,
    and he will make your paths straight.

PROVERBS 3:5-6

Whether you turn to the right or to the left, your ears
will hear a voice behind you, saying, "This is the way;
walk in it."

ISAIAH 30:21

You will seek me and find me when you seek me with
all your heart.

JEREMIAH 29:13

Come to me, all you who are weary and burdened,
and I will give you rest.

MATTHEW 11:28

The thief comes only to steal and kill and destroy;
I have come that they may have life, and have it to the
full.

JOHN 10:10

Jesus answered, "I am the way and the truth and the
life. No one comes to the Father except through me."

JOHN 14:6

I have told you these things, so that in me you may
have peace. In this world you will have trouble. But
take heart! I have overcome the world.

JOHN 16:33

"No eye has seen, no ear has heard,
    and no mind has imagined
what God has prepared
    for those who love him."

But it was to us that God revealed these things by his Spirit. For his Spirit searches out everything and shows us God's deep secrets.

I CORINTHIANS 2:9-10, NLT

There are different kinds of spiritual gifts, but the same Spirit is the source of them all. There are different kinds of service, but we serve the same Lord. God works in different ways, but it is the same God who does the work in all of us.

    A spiritual gift is given to each of us so we can help each other.

I CORINTHIANS 12:4-7, NLT

If any of you lacks wisdom, you should ask God, who gives generously to all without finding fault, and it will be given to you.

JAMES 1:5

You do not have because you do not ask God.

JAMES 4:2

God's Provision

Each morning I bring my requests to you and wait expectantly.

PSALM 5:3, NLT

I say to the LORD, "You are my Lord;
    apart from you I have no good thing."

PSALM 16:2

Praise be to the Lord, to God our Savior,
    who daily bears our burdens.

PSALM 68:19

Our Father in heaven,
hallowed be your name,
your kingdom come,
your will be done,
    on earth as it is in heaven.
Give us today our daily bread.
And forgive us our debts,
    as we also have forgiven our debtors.
And lead us not into temptation,
    but deliver us from the evil one.

MATTHEW 6:9-13

"Daughter, be encouraged! Your faith has made you
well." And the woman was healed at that moment.

MATTHEW 9:22, NLT

The Sabbath was made for man, not man for the Sabbath.
So the Son of Man is Lord even of the Sabbath.

MARK 2:27-28

Don't worry about anything; instead, pray about
everything. Tell God what you need, and thank him
for all he has done.

PHILIPPIANS 4:6, NLT

ACKNOWLEDGMENTS

A DREAM BEGINS in one imagination but can come into being only through the steadfast belief of many others.

One night in early 2008 during a women's retreat, I leaned over to my friend Carrie and whispered a dream in her ear. I told her I thought that—maybe someday—I could teach and write about Jesus and why he makes everything in life make sense. Carrie believed in me, and that's one of the reasons you are holding this book. Thanks also to Melissa and Lisa, who let me complain for only a little while before they remind me of the truth and bring me back to reality. There aren't enough words in the dictionary to make sense of all you three mean to me.

My name might go on the cover, but there is a huge team behind this book—Sandra and Chip, Jan and Sarah, Kim and Jillian—and all the other people behind you—*all the love*. Thanks for the opportunities and for listening to me. I thank you most of all because I know you pray for me and for *Brave Enough*. Every book is a miracle, and we get to celebrate this one together!

The book development team thought it would be a great

idea to create a DVD curriculum while I was still writing, which was actually crazytown in the best possible way. To AJ, creative genius—you share your talent and heart so generously, plus you are ridiculously amazing and my kids love you. When you told me "I learned so much" after filming every interview and every teaching session—every woman in the room fell a little in love with you. To Drew, Tyler, Chris, Chelsea, Brianna, Jes P., and Stacie—so much love. To the Isenbergs, who gave us their house for the filming—thank you! We especially loved the alpacas, even though they refused to let us ride them for the *Brave Enough* trailer.

So many women shared their stories for *Brave Enough*, but I'm particularly indebted to Olivia, Jes W., Laura, Melinda, Lizzie, Paige, Maria, and Lisa, who agreed to be interviewed. You guys embody true grace and are a gift to this project—I'm so honored by the brave and vulnerable ways you shared your stories.

To Hope, my church family: You are where I learn all the best things about being together, about receiving and giving grace, about experiencing the Kingdom of God right here on earth. A special thanks to David and Pete, whom I love so dearly and who have opened up doors for me that I never dreamed possible. No one pioneers alone.

My kids—Charlie, Cameron, and Desmond—you put up with a lot from this momma. You three make me so proud, my heart feels like it might stretch right out of my body. Each of you is so brave in your own way—and in you I see the grace of God in action. I am so honored I get to be your mom.

Finally, Dave—the love of my life—you believe in my dreams with such steadfast assurance. You withstand the ups and downs of this life together with great courage, and you always make me laugh. Thanks for letting me share our life with so many.

Finally, there is only one thing that matters:

Jesus is everything.

He makes me brave.

ENDNOTES

INTRODUCTION

1. I found this definition at http://en.wikipedia.org/wiki/Courage which cites John M. Cooper and D. S. Hutchinson, "The Republic" in *Plato: Complete Works* (Indianapolis, IN: Hackett Publishing Company, 1997), 2061–2075.

CHAPTER 1: BRAVE ENOUGH

1. *Merriam-Webster's Collegiate Dictionary*, 11th ed., s.v. "courage."
2. "Maya Angelou on Facing Evil," Caged Bird Legacy, LLC, http://www .mayaangelou.com/media/bill-moyers/.

CHAPTER 3: BRAVE-ENOUGH WOMEN EMBRACE SPIRITUAL SURVIVAL SKILLS

1. See John 6:35 and John 7:37-38.
2. Peter Kreeft, *You Can Understand the Bible* (San Francisco: Ignatius Press, 2005), xvi.
3. See Matthew 16:24 and Luke 9:23, 59.
4. Kreeft, *You Can Understand the Bible*, xv.
5. Herman Bavinck, *Reformed Dogmatics*, ed. John Bolt, vol. 3, *Sin and Salvation in Christ* (Grand Rapids, MI: Baker Academic, 2006), 328.
6. Brother Lawrence, *The Practice of the Presence of God*, trans. John J. Delaney (New York: Doubleday, 1977), 51.
7. Michael Comins, "Elijah and the 'Still, Small Voice,'" *Torah Trek: The Center for Jewish Wilderness Spirituality*, http://www.torahtrek.org/app-writings /writing-2.
8. Alicia Britt Chole, *Intimate Conversations: Devotions to Nurture a Woman's Soul* (Grand Rapids, MI: Revell, 2009), 178.

CHAPTER 4: BRAVE-ENOUGH WOMEN LOVE GRACE

1. Matthew 9:20-22
2. Acts 7:57–8:3
3. Read the story of Paul (also known as Saul) in Acts 9.

4. *Hebrew-Greek Key Word Study Bible*, NIV edition (1996), ed. Spiros Zodhiates, s.v. "charis."

CHAPTER 5: BRAVE-ENOUGH WOMEN GIVE GRACE

1. As quoted in *Spirituality and Liberation: Overcoming the Great Fallacy* by Robert McAfee Brown (Louisville, KY: Westminster Press, 1988), 136.
2. Dana Crowley Jack, "Understanding Women's Anger: A Description of Relational Patterns," 2001, http://faculty.wwu.edu/djack/publications /Understanding_Women's_Anger.pdf.
3. Ibid.
4. Findings attributed to S. P. Thomas, *Women and Anger*, mentioned in Melissa Dittmann, "Anger Across the Gender Divide," *Monitor on Psychology*, vol. 34, no. 3 (March 2003): 52, http://www.apa.org/monitor/mar03/angeracross.aspx.
5. John Mark McMillan, "How He Loves," copyright © 2009. This song has been covered by several Christian artists, including the David Crowder Band.

CHAPTER 6: BRAVE-ENOUGH WOMEN DON'T FEAR A FIGHT

1. See, for example, 2 Corinthians 5:18-19: "All this is from God, who reconciled us to himself through Christ and gave us the ministry of reconciliation: that God was reconciling the world to himself in Christ, not counting people's sins against them. And he has committed to us the message of reconciliation."
2. See John 18:10.
3. The phrase "tender and mild" to describe Jesus is from the Christmas carol "Silent Night"—not from Scripture.

CHAPTER 7: BRAVE-ENOUGH WOMEN EXPLORE THEIR TERRITORY

1. Scripture often speaks to us as individual members of the body of Christ, designed to bring God's message to the world. See Romans 7:4; 1 Corinthians 12; Ephesians 4:12.
2. *Merriam-Webster's Collegiate Dictionary*, 11th ed., s.v. "serendipity."
3. Dictionary.com, s.v. "vocation," http://dictionary.reference.com/browse /vocation.
4. Although this is my own definition, I am indebted to a variety of Christian thinkers who have helped me understand calling. Please see Parker Palmer, *Let Your Life Speak* (San Francisco: Jossey-Bass, 2000) and Os Guinness, *The Call* (Nashville: Thomas Nelson, 2003) for further reading.
5. Parker Palmer, *A Hidden Wholeness: The Journey toward an Undivided Life* (San Francisco: Jossey-Bass, 2004), 58.
6. David and I cohost a podcast every week called *Becoming*, which is a free download on iTunes. To hear more about this topic, download the episode entitled "The Kingdom of Self."
7. Parker Palmer, *Let Your Life Speak* (San Francisco: Jossey-Bass, 2000), 4.
8. Ibid., 5.

CHAPTER 8: BRAVE-ENOUGH WOMEN KNOW THEIR LIMITS

1. Galatians 5:25
2. "Antiaging Products and Services: The Global Market," press release, *MarketWatch*, August 19, 2013, http://www.marketwatch.com/story/antiaging-products-and-services-the-global-market-2013-08-19.
3. Meredith Lepore, "15 Facts about Starbucks That Will Blow Your Mind," *Business Insider*, March 25, 2011, http://www.businessinsider.com/15-facts-about-starbucks-that-will-blow-your-mind-2011-3?op=1.
4. *Hebrew-Greek Key Word Study Bible*, NIV edition (1996), ed. Spiros Zodhiates, s.v. "sabbat."
5. Dasee Berkowitz, "In Experiencing Real Freedom, the Importance of Boundaries," *JTA*, March 11, 2013, http://www.jta.org/2013/03/11/life-religion/in-experiencing-real-freedom-the-importance-of-boundaries#ixzz3DTG0wPrN.
6. Ian Morgan Cron, "Prayer," https://www.youtube.com/watch?v=qYHLwAIDxtM.
7. A Hasidic proverb quoted in Parker J. Palmer, *The Courage to Teach: Exploring the Inner Landscape of a Teacher's Life* (San Francisco: Jossey-Bass, 1998), 110.

CHAPTER 9: OUR DAILY BRAVE

1. *Hebrew-Greek Key Word Study Bible*, NIV edition (1996), ed. Spiros Zodhiates, s.v. "hagios."
2. Elisabeth Elliot, *Let Me Be a Woman* (Carol Stream, IL: Tyndale, 1976), 43.
3. 1 Thessalonians 5:23, *Phillips*

For more resources to help you start living a brave-enough life—including exclusive videos, downloads, and a small group study guide—visit

www.GetBraveEnough.com

ABOUT THE AUTHOR

NICOLE UNICE is a fresh voice for the next generation. Part Bible teacher, part community organizer, and part busy mom, Nicole has the uncanny ability to relate to people of all ages and in all stages of life with her "keeping it real" approach to ordering life around God's Word.

Through her writing and speaking ministries, Nicole has a wide reach. Her first book, *She's Got Issues*, released in May 2012, speaks to a fundamental question of faith: Is being a Christian supposed to change me? Also available is a companion curriculum, *She's Got Issues DVD Group Experience*, a six-week journey of interviews, questions, and teaching expanding on the book.

Nicole's invitations to speak have taken her across the country to conferences and women's retreats, big and small. Her heart belongs to Hope Church in Richmond, Virginia, where she serves as a ministry director, directing Praxis, a full-time internship program, and supporting the mission and vision of Hope.

You can catch her podcasting every Tuesday with senior pastor David Dwight. They spend fifteen minutes talking about "God's truth and modern life" and laughing about all kinds of other things. David and Nicole have coauthored a new book called *Start Here: Beginning a Relationship with Jesus*, which released in April 2014.

Nicole received her undergraduate degree in psychology from the College of William and Mary and her master's in Christian counseling from Gordon-Conwell Theological Seminary. She loves creating space for ministry and spiritual formation in the everyday rhythms of life with her awesome husband, Dave, and their three kids.

Nicole is known for making friends in all corners of the world, especially via social media. Connect with her on Facebook or via Twitter—and hopefully face-to-face at one of her upcoming events.

Bring *Brave Enough* to your
community, and start living

BOLD and FREE

Brave Enough

Find the courage to be who
you are . . . not who you wish
you were. Discover what it
means to live a brave-enough
life, fully alive and confident
in who God made you to be.

978-1-4964-0136-6

Brave Enough DVD Group Experience

Join Nicole on an eight-week
journey to being brave enough
right where you are.

978-1-4964-0138-0

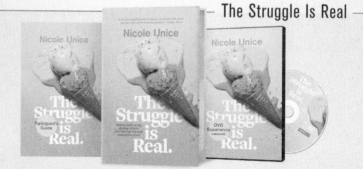